The Theory of Development Finance

ENTWICKLUNG UND FINANZIERUNG
DEVELOPMENT AND FINANCE

Herausgegeben von/Edited by
Manfred Nitsch, Reinhard H. Schmidt und Claus-Peter Zeitinger

Bd./Vol. 11

PETER LANG
Frankfurt am Main · Berlin · Bern · Bruxelles · New York · Oxford · Wien

Ingo Tschach

The Theory of Development Finance

How Microcredit Programmes Alleviate Credit and Labour Market Segmentation

PETER LANG
Europäischer Verlag der Wissenschaften

Die Deutsche Bibliothek - CIP-Einheitsaufnahme

Tschach, Ingo:

The theory of development finance : how microcredit programmes alleviate credit and labour market segmentation / Ingo Tschach. - Frankfurt am Main ; Berlin ; Bern ; Bruxelles ; New York ; Oxford ; Wien : Lang, 2002
(Development and Finance ; Vol. 11)
Zugl.: Frankfurt (Main), Univ., Diss., 2000
ISBN 3-631-39203-6

D 30
ISSN 0946-0209
ISBN 3-631-39203-6
US-ISBN 0-8204-5493-1

www.peterlang.de

Foreword

High quality academic research has to meet four criteria. It ought to deal with important topics; it has to generate new results and insights; it must be well researched; and it should be presented in a way which enables competent readers to understand the entire argument, and to assess the validity of the results. The present study by Dr. Ingo Tschach meets all four criteria to an unusually high degree. In my view, it is exactly what its title indicates: *the* theory of microfinance, i.e. the first attempt to present a consistent account of why microfinance is important to solve a serious economic problem.

The topic of the study is extremely important from a development policy point of view and thus for policy makers, practitioners and ultimately to the millions of people who are affected by the quality of development policy efforts in the field of small-enterprise finance. Imperfections and segmentation in financial and labour markets in developing and so-called transition countries are among the most serious obstacles to a sound economic and social development. Market imperfections reduce the opportunities, and undermine the incentives, for acting in an entrepreneurial manner: why should any person with energy and talent bother to create a small enterprise and strive to make it grow if he or she can foresee that the existing structure of credit and labour markets would pose insurmountable obstacles to any effort of eventually transforming a small firm into a mid-sized firm? It is important to understand precisely the nature and the effects of these obstacles if one aspired to remove them, as has been tried in the context of thousands of aid projects during the last fifty years.

The understanding of the importance, and the imperfections, of financial markets in developing countries among practitioners and politicians has greatly advanced over the past two decade. As a consequence, practical efforts to solve these problems have, by and large, also become more appropriate and, at least in a number of cases also more successful. But from an analytical point of view, the level of understanding of what is wrong with these markets and what consequences this entails, is still deficient. This lack of a "secure" intellectual basis for the practical efforts in this field manifests itself not only in the large number of projects which still fail in spite of all the good intentions, but also in the surprising degree of "ad-hocery" and emotionality with which fundamental questions are typically discussed. It often seems as if they were a matter of religious conviction.

In his study, Dr. Tschach addresses the following questions: Why is capital market segmentation in developing economies so pervasive? How are capital market segmentation and labour market segmentation related, and what does this dual segmentation imply for income distribution? What kinds of efforts exist to overcome this segmentation, and how can microfinance affect and improve this situation? And how can the potential impact of microfinance institutions on income, growth and, most of all, income distribution be assessed?

These questions and the answers provided in the present study build upon each other quite naturally. This corresponds to the practical interest of those working in this field. Many of them want to know why they do what they are doing even if they feel that what they do makes sense and may even be successful. The study provides guidance for practical work, not in the sense of a cookbook, but in the sense of a guide to the right questions to be asked and the relevant arguments to be invoked when one has to make decisions.

Does the study lead to new results and insights? Of course, several of the substantial results in this book are not new for those who have participated in the relevant discussions of the last years. Equally, most of the theoretical models which Dr. Tschach employs in his work are standard workhorses of economic theory. Nevertheless, the work of Ingo Tschach is completely innovative in so far as these tools and models have never been used to address the general issue of why microfinance is important.

As far as I know, there is, up until today, no unified theory of microfinance which could claim to be called a theory. There are not even any attempts to provide a strictly theoretical account of what microfinance can contribute to overcoming credit market imperfections, let alone a theoretical model which integrates the analysis of financial and labour market segmentation. The "theoretical impact analysis" in the concluding chapter of the present study ventures into genuine intellectual virgin territory, which needs to be explored simply because policy makers and practitioners of all persuasions are eager to see the "impact" of their efforts to support microfinance. This study provides the answer: microfinance creates not only opportunities, but also incentives, to make successful firms grow, and thus to create potentially successful firms in the first place.

Are the results derived in a serious and accessible way? The readers will have to judge by themselves; and they will see a uniquely consistent approach of modelling first the problems and then the solutions and finally the standards to assess the solutions. The fact that the results in this study are carefully derived from models with which all theoretically inclined economist should be familiar, and developed from clearly stated and highly plausible assumptions is more than a way of demonstrating an economist's professional acumen. It has practical relevance too. As we cannot make many large-scale experiments in the social sciences, we need other standards to assess arguments and propositions; and one way of distinguishing trash from value is to check whether a result is derived from sound assumptions. Thus the careful elaboration of a firm foundation gives weight to the propositions; and it might even help to overcome the tendency to follow fads and to propagate personal beliefs which, until today, characterises most of the relevant discourse among practitioners and even in the academic literature in this field.

Are the analysis and the results well presented, and would it be possible for readers to identify weaknesses? The study does not claim to be easy reading. But the general line of argument is crystal-clear, not least because Dr. Tschach's quest for rigor prevents him from making the common kind of comments in passing. The more technical arguments and the models are very carefully developed and explained so that no reader has to "believe" the author when he follows him on his intellectual journey.

It is indeed worth the effort to follow the author on the entire journey. In my view, Ingo Tschach has made the most important academic contribution to the debate about microfinance to date. It is not only, and not even primarily, a contribution to the discourse among academics who want to gain an understanding of an important real-world phenomenon, but also to that of the policy makers and practitioner who want to, and indeed have to, make informed decisions in the course of their work and who will, hopefully, need to know the right questions and some of the answers when they discuss their decisions with others. This is why we, as the editors of this series, appreciate the opportunity to make Dr. Tschach's work available to a broader audience interested in understanding the foundations, and in improving the practice, of development finance.

Reinhard H. Schmidt, September 2001

CONTENTS

List of Figures

Part I:

Part II:

PART III:

PART IV:

List of Tables

Introduction

In most "developing countries",[1] large segments of the population live in poverty. They work in informal small or micro enterprises which must rely on extremely expensive informal loans to meet their financing requirements. Because capital is expensive, the operations of such enterprises are highly labour intensive, and labour efficiency is low; thus, rates of pay in the informal sector are also very low. Many of these informal businesses produce non-tradable goods and services.

"Developing countries" also have a modern, formal sector which operates parallel to the informal sector and which, by comparison, has a good supply of relatively cheap capital, high labour productivity, and high rates of pay. Large factor price differentials create a wide gap between rich and poor in these countries, although they do not, as traditional economic theory predicts, lead to a high degree of factor mobility, which would tend to reduce differences in factor prices.

Economic theory has so far been unable to explain why it is that, even in countries where far-reaching liberalisation measures have made markets relatively competitive, factor markets remain segmented. In any case, the refusal on the part of formal financial institutions to offer small loans to informal-sector enterprises has been justified by pointing to interest rate ceilings (which in the meantime have been largely eliminated) or asymmetric information problems. However, banks also seldom lend even to medium-sized enterprises. Moreover, the interest rate differentials between the smallest bank loans and the largest informal loans are striking. At present, there is no clear explanation as to why no formal institutions have been established to bridge this gap by offering loans which are smaller than those available from banks at somewhat higher interest rates than those charged by banks.

The author gratefully acknowledges the substantial support of Internationale Projekt Consult (IPC) GmbH, Frankfurt.

1 "Developing countries" are understood to be countries which, in comparison with industrialised countries, have a relatively low per capita income. The term implies that there are also "developed countries" – namely, the industrialised countries – which have undergone an evolutionary process which "developing countries" should strive to duplicate. The author does not share this view. However, as there is no better term for this group of countries, it is used throughout the study, although it always appears in quotation marks to remind the reader that the choice of words is misleading.

There is also no conclusive explanation for the existence of labour market segmentation. One hypothesis holds that formal enterprises, with their limited capital resources and relatively capital-intensive production processes, cannot provide enough employment to go around, making it necessary for those left without formal-sector jobs to work in the informal sector. However, this does not explain why some enterprises do not select a combination of factors that lies somewhere between that used by formal enterprises and that which is characteristic of informal businesses. This would enable them to employ more labour with a given quantity of capital, which in turn would cause average labour productivity, and thus overall output, to rise (in comparison with the levels achieved with the existing, "segmented" mode of production). No one has been able to provide a clear answer to the question of why market forces lead to an inefficient allocation of factors of production.

Although the aforementioned questions remain open, an instrument has nonetheless been developed which, depending on one's ideological orientation, should be used either to fight poverty or to reduce the degree of segmentation in the credit market. *Poverty-oriented* small-scale credit programmes are designed to grant cheaper loans than are available in the informal sector, in particular to the poorest of the poor, and thus to reduce not only the extent of poverty, but also the injustice of prevailing lending practices; *financial market-oriented* small-scale credit programmes are intended to reduce segmentation in the credit market by deepening the financial sector. Indeed, institutions have been established which grant small and micro-loans at achieve, or come close to achieving, cost coverage. There seems to be no doubt that these successful small loan programmes have exclusively beneficial effects. However, impact analyses of small credit programmes are limited to the direct effect on borrowers; indirect effects, e.g. on the income of small and micro entrepreneurs who have not received credit, or the development of market prices, have thus far not been analysed.

In discussing issues relating to lending, this book invariably views things from the perspective of the credit institutions, as they are the limiting side of the market. Unless explicitly defined otherwise, the "total costs of the bank" and their components are invariably understood to be the costs of lending expressed as a percentage of the loan amount.

In Part I, it is demonstrated that asymmetric information in connection with high transaction costs constitutes a *sufficient condition* for the emergence and continued existence of segmentation in the credit market. Banks cannot assess with an adequate degree of certainty either the ability or the willingness of potential borrowers to repay their loans, and thus lend only to enterprises which meet certain minimum size requirements. This does not imply that there could not also be other sufficient conditions for the existence of credit market segmentation, e.g. bureaucratic obstacles to formalisation or the imposition of overly strict requirements and financial burdens on informal enterprises wishing to formalise their operations. However, successfully addressing information- or transaction cost-related problems is *one* prerequisite for reducing segmentation in credit markets.

Part II examines the impacts of credit market segmentation, and begins by showing that segmentation in the credit market gives rise to a size-based segmentation of the enterprise sector, which in turn leads to segmented labour markets. Likewise, the segmentation of credit *and* labour markets results in a loss of efficiency within the economy as a whole, as well as in an extremely uneven distribution of income. The system is stable in politico-economic terms, despite the fact that two goals which usually involve a trade-off – namely equitable income distribution and growth – are rendered complementary.

Part III describes how successful small-scale lending programmes solve the problems outlined in Part I. It starts with an analysis of the significance of the domestic supply of savings, which is followed by a discussion of the effects of individual measures to increase borrowers' ability and willingness to repay their loans. Subsequently, the specific combinations of these measures which are typically implemented by various types of institutions – as well as the competitive advantages and disadvantages associated with each combination – are described.

Part IV explores the impacts which successful small-scale credit programmes have on the economy as a whole, with the various alternative institutional approaches to lending being considered separately. It begins by investigating the impacts of these programmes on the financial sector, on the size distribution of enterprises, on the labour market and on the sectoral distribution of economic activities, and then continues with an analysis of the income-related effects for borrowers, for enterprises which have not received small loans, and for consumers. Part IV concludes with a discussion of the conditions under which successful small-scale lending can lead to a worsening of a country's terms of trade, and even to welfare losses.

The Method Used

The *theoretical* arguments presented in this study are based on graphic analyses. The position and shape of the curves reflect numerous assumptions with respect to behaviour which either correspond to the tenets of traditional economic theory, or are based on plausible hypotheses and data drawn from observation of actual situations which are subsequently discussed in detail. Using this method permits one to derive conclusions which are precisely congruent with phenomena very commonly encountered in many "developing countries", and which have so far been explained only inadequately, if at all.

In most cases, no empirical evidence was provided. This was intentional. An in-depth analysis would have to take into account, and thus correctly assess, a great number of concomitant effects (see Part IV). However, this poses serious problems, as small-scale credit programmes are built up over a period of decades. Because major changes take place in their overall operating environment during this time frame, it is virtually impossible to factor out properly all exogenous "random disturbances". In any case, such an undertaking would clearly have been beyond the scope of this study. For the same reason, case studies are seldom used – here, too, external circumstances affect the results, and different cases could be used to "prove" or "reject" the validity of opposing views. Given the large number of existing case studies, it would indeed be possible to confirm all theoretically derived *direct* effects; however, the author chose not to do so in order to preserve the integrity of the study. The proposed *indirect* effects have not been captured by any existing empirical studies.

This study is intended for readers who are already familiar with the literature on small-scale credit programmes. The basics of development finance, which are discussed in depth in numerous publications, are not presented here, on the one hand to avoid covering (more general) topics with which many readers are already familiar, and on the other, to maintain the intended focus of the present study. However, it is assumed that the reader will be able to follow the arguments presented in this study without an extensive knowledge of the development finance literature.

Part I. The Theoretical Derivation of Credit Market Segmentation

Part I takes up the question of why credit market segmentation occurs. Are there "compelling" factors which make its existence inevitable? Under what conditions does segmentation take place?

In the relevant literature, credit market segmentation is attributed in part to legal interest rates ceilings, and in part to information asymmetries which can result in implicit upper limits on interest rates. Both of these factors create a situation in which formal-sector institutions grant only large loans; small borrowers are subject to credit rationing and must therefore obtain loans in the informal financial market at far higher interest rates.

In most countries, however, statutory interest rate ceilings have been eliminated, or are no longer a constraint. In theory at least, all banks can grant small and medium-sized loans at higher interest rates, although in practice they rarely do. Moreover, the literature does not explain why no institutions have emerged which offer medium-sized loans at "medium" interest rates. If such institutions existed, credit market segmentation would not occur. Instead, there would be a continuum of lending rates which would be a function of the intermediation costs and loan amounts involved in each case.

To facilitate answering this question, "enterprise size" is explicitly incorporated as a dimension of the analysis. Rather than making the typical distinction between "large" and "small" enterprises, it will represent a continuum of possible sizes. On the one hand, this will enable us to describe more clearly the causes of credit rationing and credit market segmentation; on the other, it will lay the conceptual groundwork which will be used to illustrate why there are no institutions which cater for the demand of "medium-sized" borrowers, how this impacts on the economy as a whole, and what can be done to improve the situation over the long term.

The first chapter contains a presentation of the basic model and the assumptions on which it is based. The second chapter examines how banks respond when information asymmetries prevent them from making a relatively reliable estimate of the *ability* of individual borrowers to repay their loans. The third chapter explores the banks' response to the possible or purported *unwillingness* of borrowers to pay. Both of these chapters form the basis for the derivation of a credit supply function for banks in the fourth chapter. This function will be compared with the supply function of informal lenders to demonstrate why credit market segmentation inevitably occurs.

1. The basic model and its underlying assumptions

It is often observed that the RoI of an enterprise depends on its size. The RoI of very large enterprises is relatively low because there are virtually no restrictions on the international mobility of capital for large-scale projects, and yield advantages are quickly noticed by other market participants, who then take steps to exploit such advantages for themselves.[2] By contrast, smaller enterprises can move into, and develop, narrow market niches without attracting the attention of direct competitors on the same scale. This in turn enables them to achieve higher returns than those earned by large enterprises. In addition, in nearly all "developing countries" the opportunity costs of (unskilled) labour are very low; as a result, the RoI of small and micro enterprises is extremely high, and can easily exceed 100 percent per month.[3]

These observations form the point of departure for the following analysis. It will be assumed that an enterprise's RoI decreases as its size increases. The total assets of an enterprise will be taken as a measure of its size. This correlation is shown in Figure 1, using a logarithmic scale for the X-axis. Of course, the RoI function is not a precise mirror of enterprise size; rather, it represents a broad range of possible values, for which it could constitute a line of regression.

We must now determine the costs which banks incur by lending to enterprises of various sizes. It is assumed that the size of loan demanded by an enterprise is proportional to its size.[4] Because certain transaction costs are fixed – i.e. they have no relationship to the size of the loan disbursed – the banks' costs of lending, expressed as a percentage of the loan amount, are higher for small credits than for larger ones. The risk-related costs (likewise expressed as a percentage of the loan amount) are also higher for small borrowers than for larger ones, although not because their business activities inherently involve higher risk – indeed, the opposite is true – but rather because conventional banks, with their traditional procedures, are not able to assess accurately the risk inherent in lending to such enterprises, which typically do not even keep written

---

2 This may be different in certain high-tech sectors such as computer chip production or the software or aircraft industries, owing to high market entry barriers. In the majority of "developing countries", however, businesses wishing to produce the goods supplied by most "large enterprises" do not face especially high market entry barriers.

3 Cf. SCHMIDT/MOMMARTZ, 1996, App. B4/a, p. 19.

4 Indeed, it has been observed that small and micro enterprises finance a far larger share of their "balance sheet total" internally than do large enterprises. For the sake of simplicity, in the following it will be assumed that all enterprises have the same capital ratio. If the lower capital ratios of large enterprises were taken into account in the analysis, there would be no qualitative change, and the quantitative effects would be amplified.

accounts. The purpose of a given loan has no bearing on the bank's funding costs, which are thus the same for all loans.

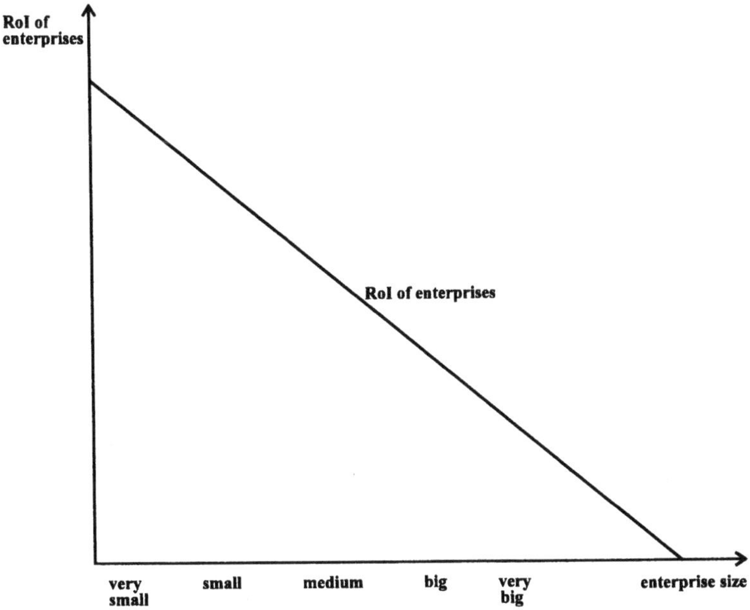

Fig. 1: The correlation between RoI and enterprise size

Figure 2 shows the costs of lending incurred by banks (expressed as a percentage of the loan amount) as a function of the size of the loan, and thus of the enterprise size. First, the banks' variable and fixed transaction costs must be added to the funding rate, i^{fund}. The transaction costs for small loan amounts can be extremely high because the loans in question are usually enterprise loans. Micro entrepreneurs usually do not qualify for other types of credit such as personal loans or overdraft facilities on current accounts, and thus have no choice but to take out enterprise loans, which are more expensive for banks to grant. The relevant risk costs have also been taken into account.

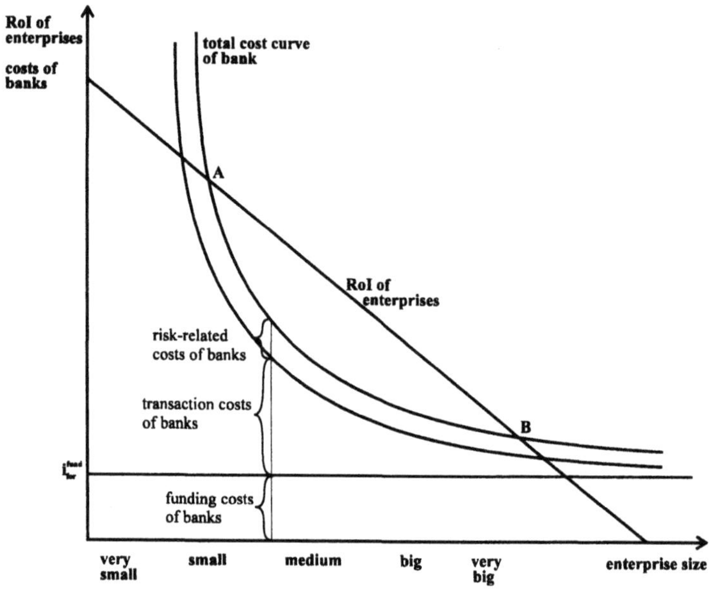

Fig. 2: The costs of lending for banks

The uppermost curve represents the costs of lending for banks as a function of the size of the loans or of the size of the borrowing enterprises. In other words, if banks lend at the interest rates on this curve, they will only just be able to cover their costs. Consequently, bank credits would be available to all enterprises for which the RoI lies above the cost curve of the banks – in other words, enterprises larger than A and smaller than B. Such an allocation of credit would also be efficient at the macro-economic level.

This model illustrates clearly the effects of statutory interest rate ceilings (Figure 3). For example, if the government introduces an interest rate ceiling of i^{max}_{legal}, enterprises will only be eligible to borrow if they generate costs of less than i^{max}_{legal} for the banks, which means they must be at least as large as SE^{min}_{for}. All enterprises smaller than SE^{min}_{for} are subject to credit rationing because the banks would lose money by lending to these businesses at an interest rate of i^{max}_{legal}. This is worthy of note in particular because the larger enterprises in this segment show the greatest spread between RoI and capital costs; i.e. from a macro-economic point of view, they are making the most efficient use of the capital available to them.

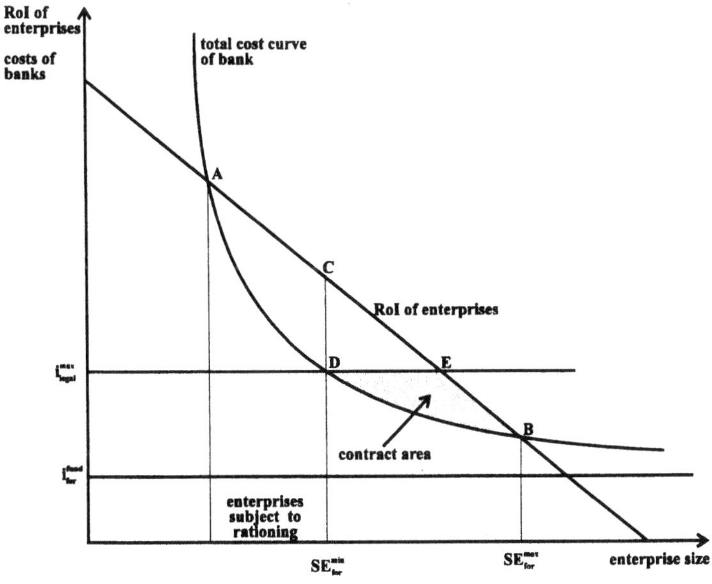

Fig. 3: The effect of legal interest rate restrictions

Thus, an area emerges within the credit market (area DEB) in which a loan contract is of absolute advantage for all participants (henceforth, this area will be referred to as the "contract area"). A contract on one of the boundaries will enable only one party to realise the maximum possible return, while the other party remains indifferent. For an enterprise of a given size, the greater the vertical distance between the "contract point" and the respective party's cost function or yield point, the higher the profits for that party will be. If this distance is multiplied by the loan amount (a function of the size of the enterprise), the result is the absolute profit for each party to the contract. The graph illustrates that an interest rate ceiling has no influence on the lending rates offered to large enterprises, whereas for smaller enterprises which have not been subject to credit rationing, such a ceiling causes the "profit distribution" to shift in favour of the enterprises.

In the meantime, legal maximum interest rates, at least of a binding nature, have been eliminated in nearly all countries. Nonetheless, experience has shown that banks usually do not raise their interest rates beyond a certain limit, preferring instead to avoid lending to small enterprises. The reasons for this will be discussed in the following chapters.

Average return vs. marginal return on capital

Thus far, the analysis has focused on factors which the banks must consider when taking lending decisions. The banks are mainly concerned with the average RoI of enterprises as a criterion for assessing their ability to repay their loans, and as a consequence, the total capital productivity of the enterprises in question has formed the basis for the analysis.

By contrast, when entrepreneurs need to decide whether to finance an additional investment with debt, they will weigh their marginal return – i.e. the additional profits generated by their planned investments – against the marginal costs of taking out additional loans. These variables must therefore be incorporated into an analysis of credit demand.

Figure 4 compares the average RoI of enterprises with their marginal capital productivity. Sample values for enterprises' total assets were entered so as to render the logarithmic scale of the X-axis somewhat more descriptive. The marginal productivity curve intersects the X-axis at a value which is equivalent to half the value represented by the point of intersection of the average return

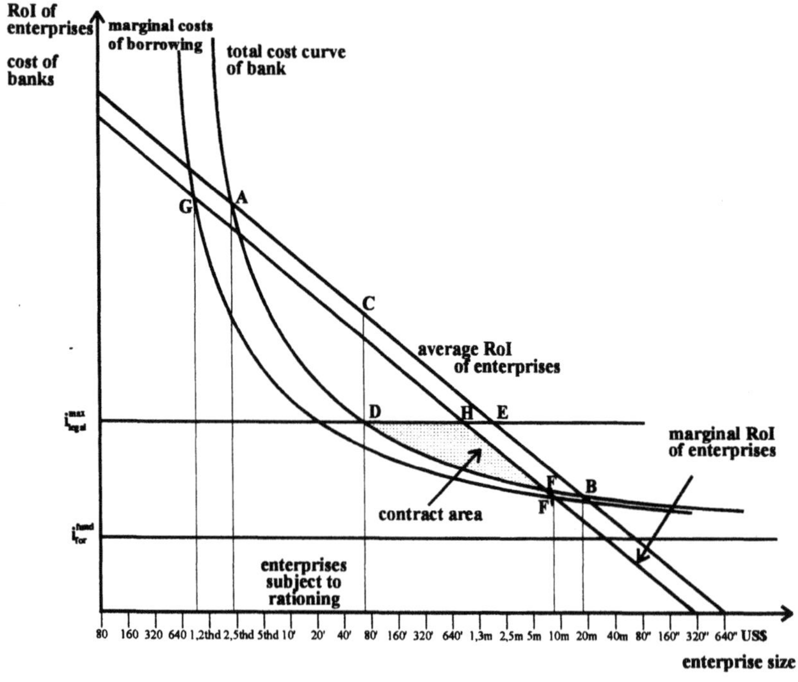

Fig. 4: Average and marginal return on capital

curve. Given the logarithmic scale, however, the point of intersection of the marginal productivity curve does not actually lie midway between the Y-axis and the average return curve but instead, as shown, is relatively close to the average return curve. The two curves are also parallel for the same reason.

The marginal costs of additional loans will be lower than the average interest costs because the interest rate will also decrease for funds borrowed anyway. The difference between the average and marginal costs of loans will decrease as the loan amount increases because the interest rate for larger loans will no longer fall by as much.

For small enterprises, the costs of financing an expansion through borrowing decrease more than their RoI, which is why a greater number of enterprises demand credit (represented by the area between A and G) in comparison with the number shown by an analysis based on average costs. However, as enterprises of this size are subject to credit rationing in any case, the extent of rationing merely increases.

By contrast, demand on the part of large enterprises diminishes. Starting at an amount of slightly less than US$ 10 million, financing an expansion with borrowed funds no longer makes economic sense. The contract area is reduced by the trapezoid HFBE (the banks continue to base their calculations on average values). However, this decline in demand for credit on the part of large enterprises has no impact on the analysis of credit market segmentation, as the latter occurs when small and medium-sized enterprises are subject to credit rationing.

Basing calculations on enterprises' average return on capital will have different implications for and effects on the market than if marginal values are used. Average returns are the relevant variable for the banks' calculations, while marginal values influence the credit demand of enterprises. In the market segments analysed in this study, applying marginal values will result in a greater credit demand than is obtained when average values are used. However, the banks, which base their calculations on average values, subject the enterprises in question to credit rationing, and thus marginal values can be ignored in the following discussion. At the same time, though, it should be borne in mind that the extent of credit demand, and thus of credit rationing, is always somewhat greater than an assessment based on average values would suggest.

2. The ability to pay and information asymmetries

This chapter analyses the impact of information asymmetries on the credit supply provided by banks. Using the STIGLITZ/WEISS (1981)[5] model, it will first be demonstrated that – like statutory regulations – asymmetric information can lead to a situation in which it would be detrimental to the banks if they were to raise interest rates above a certain level. As a result, the pricing mechanism which could serve to clear the markets is rendered ineffective. In the second part of the chapter, several highly restrictive assumptions of the STIGLITZ/WEISS model are suspended; the new conclusions yielded by the revised model are then used to derive the banks' response to information asymmetries, especially as regards pricing and rationing.

a) The Stiglitz/Weiss model

This section contains a brief summary of the key arguments presented in the article by STIGLITZ and WEISS (1981). A detailed derivation of the results will not be presented here.[6]

Figure 5 summarises the basic features of the STIGLITZ/WEISS model.[7] The third quadrant represents a savings function in which it is assumed that there is a positive correlation between savings volume (S) and the interest rate on savings deposits (r^s). However, there would be no fundamental change in the results even if the savings volume were completely inelastic with respect to interest rates. The return on the banks' lending activities (r) must be at least as high as the deposit interest rate. For the sake of simplicity, these two variables are assumed to be equal and in the following are represented by the same symbol. In the second quadrant, the savings volume is merely transposed into the first quadrant, where it represents the credit supply.[8]

---

5 Cf. STIGLITZ/WEISS, 1981.

6 For a more detailed derivation see Tschach, 1995.

7 Cf. STIGLITZ/WEISS, 1981.

8 Owing to the multiplier effect, the banks can lend amounts which are a multiple of their deposits. However, because the multiplier is an exogenous factor and thus a constant, the result is merely a bubble which is assumed to be already contained in the savings function shown on the graph.

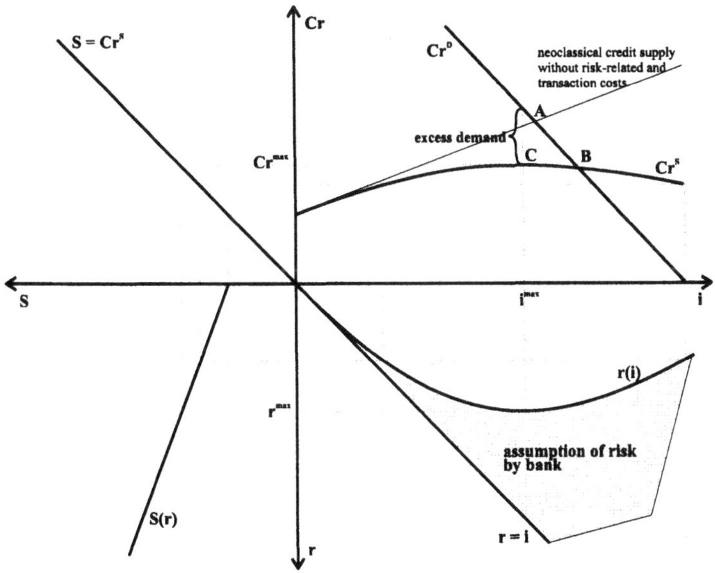

Fig. 5: The central implications of STIGLITZ/WEISS (1981)

The first and fourth quadrants are of key importance. The fourth quadrant depicts the banks' return (r) as a function of the lending interest rate (i). Proceeding from the assumption of asymmetric information distribution between lender and borrower, STIGLITZ and WEISS show, on the one hand, that when lending interest rates go up, low-risk borrowers do not (cannot) realise their projects. On the other hand, for borrowers who continue to implement projects, rising interest rates provide an incentive to invest in increasingly risky projects. The banks must bear part of the risk, which is reflected in their returns: While the straight line in the fourth quadrant describes a correlation between r and i which would apply if there were no credit risk for the bank (r = i), r(i) represents the correlation which is in fact relevant for the bank. STIGLITZ and WEISS have shown that when interest rates increase beyond a certain rate (i^{max}), the banks' returns must decrease.

The first quadrant plots the credit supply of the banks, which is depicted through simple transposition in a four-quadrant system (unlike typical representations of supply and demand, the position of the axes here has been reversed). Although there is a point at which credit supply and credit demand intersect (B), this point represents an interest rate which is higher than i^{max} (C). The banks are not willing to charge such high rates, because in doing so they would reduce their own returns. Thus, they will disburse Cr^{max} loans at an interest rate of exactly i^{max}. By "refusing" to charge higher interest rates (i.e. prices), which would in turn reduce the demand which exists at i^{max}, the banks render the market mechanism ineffective: The existing excess demand for funds cannot be absorbed by increased prices, but instead remains at the level plotted on the graph.

Thus, it may be concluded that even without legal interest rate restrictions, information asymmetries can lead to "implicit" interest rate ceilings; this in turn prevents markets from clearing and leads to credit rationing. These effects are illustrated in Figure 3, and are analogous to the impact of statutory interest rate ceilings.

b) Elaborations on the Stiglitz/Weiss model

We shall now extend the STIGLITZ/WEISS model so as to make its assumptions compatible with those of the basic model. The assumptions of STIGLITZ and WEISS which are problematic in this respect are that a) all borrowers demand credit in equal amounts, b) all borrowers have the same expected RoI on their projects, and c) no transaction costs need be taken into account.

These three assumptions shall now be refuted. Depending on their size, enterprises achieve different RoIs, demand loans of varying size, and generate varying transaction cost levels expressed as a share of the loan amount. How do these changes affect the model as depicted above?

An increase in an enterprise's expected RoI will, owing to higher anticipated profits, in principle have two effects: on the one hand, the risk borne by the banks at a given interest rate decreases (distance to the 45° line); on the other, the interest rate at which banks can maximise their returns, i^{max}, increases. As a result of these two effects, the return function for the banks, r(i), is extended down and to the right. The level of the transaction costs incurred by the banks is not a function of the interest rate charged, and, as a result, factoring in the transaction costs causes an upward parallel shift in the return function.

Fig. 6 illustrates these correlations separately for small and large loans. Small loans are granted to small enterprises with higher RoIs, and thus the return function of the banks which applies to them, $r(i)^{small}_{gross}$, is relatively flat. However, this function does not yet take into account the banks' transaction costs. Because transaction costs are relatively high for small loans, this causes a relatively strong upward shift in the return function. The net return of the banks, less transaction costs, is depicted by the function $r(i)^{small}_{net}$.

The analogous function for large loans is relatively compressed; the distance between this curve and the 45° line increases more than the function $r(i)^{small}_{net}$ as the interest rate rises. However, because the banks' transaction costs, expressed as a percentage of the loan amount, are significantly lower for large loans, the curve is not shifted upward as strongly; $r(i)^{large}_{net}$ is the function which represents the banks' net return on large loans.

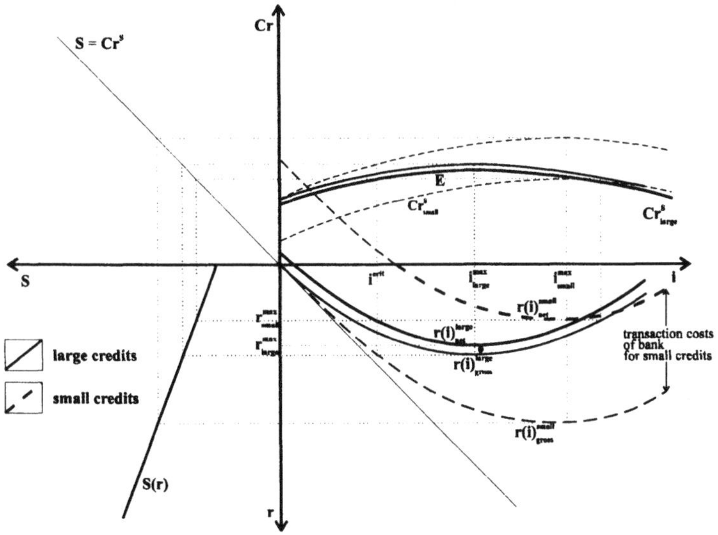

Fig. 6: The expanded STIGLITZ/WEISS model

Although the interest rate at which banks can maximise their return is substantially higher for small loans (i^{max}_{small}) than for large credits (i^{max}_{large}), it is clear that the banks' return, r(i), is nonetheless higher for large loans. The only case in which the banks' return on small loans will be comparable to what they can earn on large loans is if the interest rate in the market for large loans is lower than i^{crit}. If it is, large loans would be granted at an interest rate of i^{crit}, while small borrowers would have to pay the much higher interest rate of i^{max}_{small}. It should be noted that despite the considerable difference in interest rates, the banks' net return, r^{max}_{small}, would be identical for both groups of borrowers.

The credit supply curves transposed into the first quadrant require a great deal of interpretation. The necessary analysis will be performed on the basis of the following graph. In Figure 7, the conditions presumed above are juxtaposed with three possible credit demand functions for large borrowers. If the demand of large borrowers is equivalent to Cr^{D2}_{large}, an interest rate higher than i^{crit} will emerge in this market segment at which the banks' net return is higher than the return they could earn in the small loan market. For this reason, the banks will only grant large loans, and completely ration credit to small borrowers. If the demand for large loans corresponds to Cr^{D3}_{large}, then even large borrowers will be subject to credit rationing, because demand will also exceed the maximum possible supply at an interest rate of i^{max}_{large}.

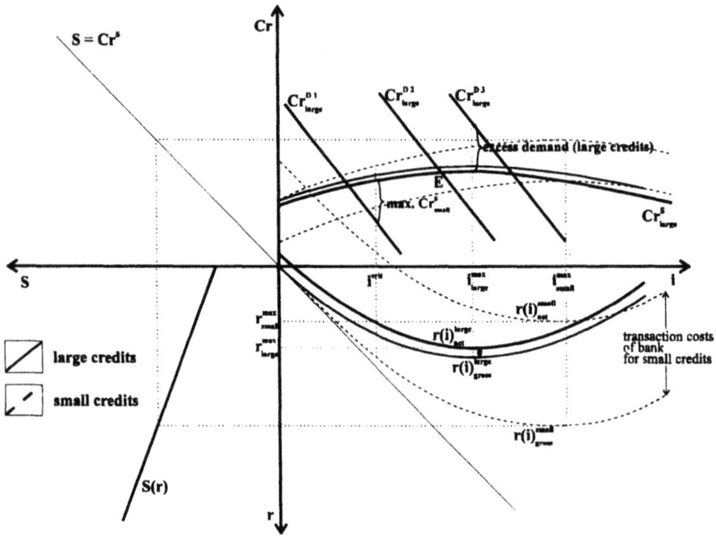

Fig. 7: The credit supply provided by banks according to the expanded STIGLITZ/WEISS model

Loans will not be offered to small borrowers at all unless the demand for large credits intersects the supply function at an interest rate which is lower than i^{crit}. In the case of the demand curve plotted here, Cr^{D1}_{large}, the credit volume available to small borrowers would correspond to the difference between supply and demand in the large loan market at an interest rate of i^{crit}. The small loans would then carry an interest rate of i^{max}_{small}. If the demand for small loans is larger than $\max Cr^{S}_{small}$, credit rationing would continue to occur in this market segment. Only if the demand is smaller than $\max Cr^{S}_{small}$ will interest rates decline for both small and large loans, and they will decline in such a way that the net return for the banks, r(i), is always the same in both segments of the market.

Thus, we can distinguish between three market situations, each of which would have different consequences for small borrowers:

a) The demand for large loans causes interest rates in this market to rise above i^{crit}, and thus no small loans are granted. The banks earn a net return which is higher than r^{max}_{small}.

b) In the market for large loans, demand intersects the supply function at an interest rate lower than i^{crit}. The banks nonetheless charge large borrowers an interest rate of i^{crit}; with the excess supply of funds from this market being lent to borrowers in the market for small loans at an interest rate of i^{max}_{small}. However, this excess supply diverted from the market for large loans is not sufficient to satisfy the demand in this market segment. Changes in supply or demand in the market for large loans have no impact whatsoever on conditions in this market; lending rates remain stable. However, given a constant interest rate of i^{max}_{small} for small loans, these changes will cause the credit supply in the market for small loans to fluctuate by precisely the same amount as the excess supply in the market for large loans, but in the opposite direction. For example, if the demand for large loans were to increase by US$ 1 million, the credit supply in the small-loan market would drop by exactly the same amount. By contrast, fluctuations in the demand for small loans will only affect the small-loan market itself, namely by varying the extent to which borrowers are subject to credit rationing. Thus, the market for small loans is dependent on the large-loan market. The banks realise a net return of exactly r^{max}_{small}.

c) The demand for small loans at an interest rate of i^{max}_{small} is smaller than the excess supply in the large-loan market at an interest rate of i^{crit}. Credit rationing no longer takes place; the banks must accept a net return of less than r^{max}_{small}. Fluctuations in demand in each of the two market segments now affect interest rates and the credit volume available in both segments, i.e. there is an interdependence between the two market segments.

c) Pricing and rationing given asymmetric information

Thus far, this chapter has made statements with respect to credit rationing only insofar as two loan sizes are concerned. As this restriction could be misleading, it will now be eliminated. As this cannot be done on the basis of the STIGLITZ/WEISS model, the preliminary results derived in the previous section will now be incorporated into the basic model.

As was shown, information asymmetries can lead to the emergence of implicit interest rate ceilings. Even in the absence of statutory regulations, these ceilings prevent banks from raising their interest rates beyond a certain level. However, the difference between implicit and statutory upper limits on interest rates is that the implicit ceilings are a function of the size of the borrowing enterprise. The smaller an enterprise, the higher its expected RoI, which, given a constant interest rate, reduces a bank's risk costs. Therefore, the interest rates at which asymmetric information begins to have a negative impact on the banks' net return are higher for small enterprises than for large ones. The implicit interest rate ceiling rises as the size of the enterprise decreases; this phenomenon is represented by an "interest rate ceiling function", which is depicted in Figure 8.

The banks must take into account the interest rate ceiling function i_{for}^{max}, which plots the interest rate at which they can maximise their return for an enterprise of any given size. Banks will thus not charge interest rates which lie above this function, nor will they lend to enterprises for which the anticipated costs exceed revenues. They will only lend to enterprises for which the total costs curve lies below the interest rate ceiling function, which is the case for enterprises of a size ranging between SE_{for}^{min} and SE_{for}^{max}. All enterprises smaller than SE_{for}^{min} will be subject to credit rationing.

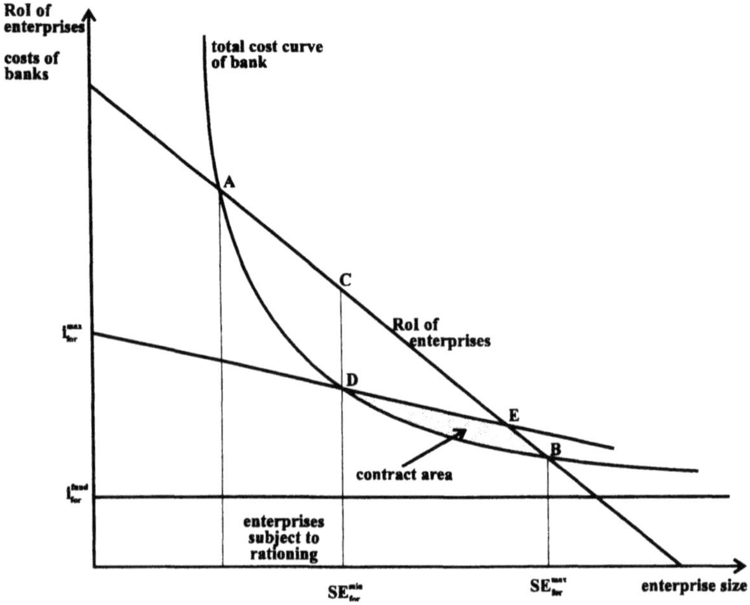

Fig. 8: The credit supply provided by banks under conditions of asymmetric information

The contract area is represented by the figure DBE. The banks will attempt to lend at rates which correspond to the points on the segments DE and EB, because this is where they will realise the highest profits. For the enterprises, interest rates corresponding to points on the DB curve would be ideal. All points between these lines represent lending rates which make credit relationships profitable for both banks and enterprises; the lending rates that actually emerge will be a function of prevailing market conditions and the extent of competition in the financial sector.

Thus, even if allowance is made for the dependence of the size of enterprises on their RoI, for transaction costs, and for the fact that there is a continuum of possible enterprise sizes, information asymmetries lead to implicit interest rate ceilings which prevent small and medium-sized enterprises from obtaining access to bank loans, despite the fact that their expected RoIs are higher (sometimes much higher) than the banks' total costs. What is efficient for an individual economic unit thus leads to inefficiencies for the economy as a whole.

3. The willingness to pay

If a loan is actually to be paid back, the borrower must not only be able, but also willing to pay. Yet why should borrowers wish to pay back their loans at all? The answer is simple: by repaying the loan, they will reap greater benefits than if they refuse to pay! In other words, they will only pay back their loans if it is advantageous for them to do so.

But why should borrowers be better off if they pay back their loans? After all, this requires a considerable sacrifice. What exactly compels a borrower to repay his or her debts?

The repayment of a loan can be motivated by *intrinsic* or *extrinsic* factors. In this context, intrinsic motivation means that borrowers pay back their loans because of their own attitudes, ethical considerations, personal relationships, etc., rather than because of economic considerations. Behaving otherwise would simply make them feel bad. In a broader sense, repaying a loan to avoid losing face is also a form of intrinsic motivation. Because borrowers' actions are noted by other persons in their social environment, they must expect social sanctions for behaviour which does not comply with social norms.

In the following, extrinsic motivation is taken to mean that a debtor pays back his loans because it is economically advantageous for him. There can be a number of reasons for this. For example, the bank might foreclose on his house, and he would lose more than he stood to gain by refusing to repay the loan; he might be denied access to subsequent loans, which for him are more valuable than the repayments that are due; the other persons or enterprises with whom he does business might stop trusting him and either refuse to do further business with him or take such extensive "safety precautions" that each transaction would become substantially more expensive. For all of these reasons, refusing to pay back a loan can be "more expensive" than repaying it, and would thus be irrational.

This chapter begins examining intrinsic motivation on the part of small borrowers based on a sociological analysis by Max Weber. In the second section, several reasons for a lack of extrinsic motivation will be presented in order to determine the impact this has on the credit supply provided by banks.

a) Intrinsic motivation and social distance

This section begins with a sociological analysis by MAX WEBER on the topic of usury, which enables us to draw conclusions regarding the factors which influence the intrinsic motivation of small borrowers to pay back their formal-sector credits.

In nearly all religions, lending at interest is considered ethically reprehensible, and is regarded as usury.[9] "Originally, lending at interest was invariably regarded with such abhorrence [..]" because of "the nature of primitive emergency loans as a response to requests for aid, which must have made charging interest 'among brothers' appear to be a violation of the obligation to help others in need."[10] The concept of neighbourly help ("A man shall help his neighbour, for he may also one day require the help of his fellows."[11]) developed into an ethical code of reciprocity within closed ethnic or religious communities.[12] Thus, the 5th book of Moses, which is regarded as a sacred text by Jews, Christians and Moslems, commands: "Thou shalt not lend upon usury to they brother; usury of money, usury of victuals, usury of any thing that is lent upon usury. Unto a stranger thou mayest lend upon usury; but unto thy brother thou shalt not lend upon usury."[13] As in all traditional societies, there was no

9 Cf. TRENK, 1991, p. 143.

10 Cf. WEBER, 1972, p. 352, own translation.

11 WEBER, 1972, p. 350, own translation.

12 Cf. TRENK, 1991, p. 143, and SIMON, 1993, pp. 63-76, on altruism in social and cultural evolution.

13 DEUTERONOMY, XXIII, 19/20

ethical universalism in Hebraic culture.[14] WEBER differentiates between internal and external morality:

> "Originally, two different attitudes towards the acquisition of worldly goods stood in sharp contrast to one another: on the one hand, within one's own circle allegiance to tradition, to a relationship of dutiful respect among members of the tribe, clan or household, which precluded unrestrained acquisition of possessions among members of the circle, who were bound to each other by ties of dutiful respect – i.e. *internal morality* – and an absolute lack of restraint with respect to the acquisition of worldly goods in dealings outside of this circle, where every stranger was originally perceived as an enemy to whom might behave as one pleased, without regard for ethical restraints – *external morality*. This state of affairs began to change when, on the one hand, the notion of calculating the relative value of things, and of keeping and settling accounts, began to take hold in dealings among members of the traditional units of social organisation, where it undermined the old ties of dutiful respect. As soon as the members of a family community began to keep and settle accounts with each other instead of managing their affairs in a strictly communal manner, the naive attitude of dutiful respect and suppression of the urge to acquire worldly goods became a thing of the past. This aspect of the evolution was especially pronounced in the West. At the same time, the unrestrained pursuit of profit was tempered when the principle of acquisition was applied to dealings in the internal economy. The result was *regulated economic activity* allowing a certain *scope for the urge to acquire*."[15]

According to NELSON[16], the abandonment of particularism in Christianity and Islam is an outgrowth of the claim made by each religion to represent a system of belief and values applicable to all of mankind. Thus, the prohibition on lending at interest was construed as applying to everyone. Later, the Protestant Reformation embraced the concept of universalism while simultaneously citing the exception enumerated in the Old Testament.[17] NELSON summarises the consequences as follows: "In short, Western morality after Calvin reaffirmed the vocabulary of universalism, refused to concede that God could authorise or equity allow us to treat the Other different from the Brother, assimilated the Brother to the Other, and eventuated in the Universal Otherhood. In modern

14 Cf. TRENK, 1991, p. 143.

15 WEBER, 1923, p. 303, own translation.

16 Cf. NELSON, 1969, p. 3f.

17 Cf. TRENK, 1991, p. 145.

capitalism, we are all 'brothers' in being equally 'others'."[18] Group members and strangers, internal and external relationships were on a par with one another. This put an end to both the ban on lending at interest as well as unrestrained acquisitiveness.[19] They were supplanted by a universal economic code of ethics.

Nonetheless, in western societies as well, the social proximity or distance of institutions continues to influence the behaviour of individuals. Thus, insurance fraud or tax evasion on a small scale is regarded by many as a petty offence; there is a vast social distance between the individual and institutions such as the government and insurance companies. By contrast, people always give friends a "special deal", because they would feel bad if they acted in accordance with purely economic considerations in their dealings with friends.

The situation is no different for small borrowers in "developing countries". The greater the social distance between the borrower and the lending institution, the less intrinsic motivation there is for the borrower to pay back the loan. Above all, people in the poorer strata of the population often consider banks to be extraneous entities that are not part of the reality of their own lives. Intrinsic motivation (in the narrow sense) to pay back bank loans thus tends to be quite low.

Because banks are subject to an "external morality" which applies to persons and entities lying outside the boundaries of the world which borrowers perceive as their own, those who refuse to pay back their loans need not fear sanctions within their immediate social environment. On the contrary, borrowers who successfully avoid repaying their loans often receive social recognition for their cunning.[20] Thus, it is highly unlikely that they would pay back their loans because of intrinsic motivation in the broader sense.

On the whole, then, borrowers who receive small loans from traditional banks can be expected to have very little intrinsic motivation to honour their loan contracts and repay loans which have already been disbursed. The banks have no choice but to acknowledge this fact; their only recourse is to ensure that borrowers meet their payment obligations by bringing extrinsic motivation to bear.

---

18 NELSON, 1969, p. XXIV.

19 Cf. TRENK, 1991, p. 145.

20 The same behaviour vis-à-vis institutions with social proximity to the lender would result in serious social sanctions. This is one reason why borrowers are more likely to pay back informal loans than formal ones (cf. ADAMS/GRAHAM, 1981, p. 352).

b) Extrinsic motivation and the implications for the credit supply of banks

There are two extrinsic factors which can motivate borrowers to repay their loans. On the one hand, they avoid costs that could arise if the bank attempts to force them to pay back their loans. On the other hand, they safeguard future benefits for themselves which can arise in the form of a continued business relationship with the bank, but which they will only be able to reap if the current credit has been repaid (intertemporal linkage).

Of course, intertemporal linkage only "works" if borrowers can in fact assume that their co-operative behaviour will in fact induce their banks to grant them access to credit in the future. However, this is seldom the case. As was shown in Section 2b, given constant interest rates, fluctuations in demand in the "large loan market" usually lead to corresponding fluctuations in supply on the "small loan market". The same mechanism naturally applies to fluctuations in supply – e.g. as a result of measures taken by the central bank – to which commercial banks respond by "regulating" the supply of funds which they are willing to lend out in the form of very small loans; larger loans are usually affected only slightly, if at all. It has thus been observed in many countries that the supply of small credits, assuming such a supply exists at all, is subject to strong fluctuations. Consequently, small borrowers have learned in the past that timely repayment of all instalments does not guarantee their personal access to credit. Intertemporal linkage therefore provides little incentive for repayment of loans to conventional banks.

Consequently, the only remaining option for the banks is to make clear that they will force borrowers to fulfil their obligations by taking legal action. In many countries, however, the banking sector is subject to laws which are designed to protect borrowers, and which grant creditors little scope for action. For them, initiating legal proceedings to collect their receivables is a very lengthy and expensive process in which the costs of the legal measures often exceed the value of the small loans involved. In addition, if legal restrictions or a given borrower's economic situation prevent the banks from passing on these legal costs to uncooperative borrowers, it makes little economic sense for them to enforce the repayment of loans through legal measures. Borrowers are also aware of this, and thus they would presumably have little, if any, extrinsic motivation to repay their loans.

As a result, banks will not grant loans if the costs generated by potential legal proceedings would exceed the loan amount. The laws which are intended to protect borrowerss thus prevent them from receiving access to credit in the first place. The more expensive it is for the banks to enforce the repayment of loans through legal action, the higher the "minimum loan amount" will be.

These points have been incorporated into the results of the preceding analysis, as shown in Figure 9. It was assumed that the costs which banks incur by taking legal action to enforce payment (the costs of foreclosure and liquidation of collateral) are equal to the size of the loan demanded by enterprises with a size of $SE^{*\,min}_{for}$. Thus, these loans would still be larger than the minimum loan amount which would emerge as a consequence of information asymmetries and the accompanying lack of opportunities to accurately assess the borrowers' ability to pay back their loans (SE^{min}_{for}).[21]

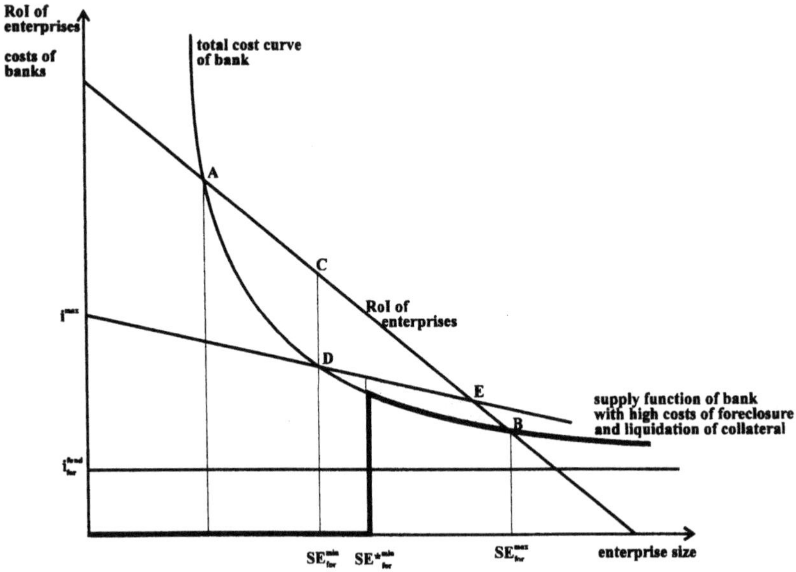

Fig. 9: Costs of foreclosure and liquidation of collateral and the credit supply of banks

As was argued above, banks will only grant loans in which the loan amount exceeds the potential costs of foreclosure and liquidation of collateral, in this case $SE^{*\,min}_{for}$. The bank's total costs function still represents the possible credit

---

21 This does not have to be the case. However, if $SE^{*\,min}_{for}$ is smaller than SE^{min}_{for}, there is no binding constraint, and further analysis is superfluous. Figure 9 thus applies to all other cases.

supply. Of course, here as well the bank will attempt – depending on market conditions – to charge higher interest rates within the contract area.

Borrowers who demand loans which are smaller than $SE^{*\,min}_{for}$ are subject to credit rationing because they would have neither intrinsic nor extrinsic motivation to pay back their loans, and are thus unattractive customers for banks. Credit is rationed not only due to asymmetric information, but also as a result of the high costs of foreclosure and liquidation of collateral. Which of these two possible causes serves as the binding constraint, and thus determines precisely where the "frontier of formal finance" lies, must be decided separately for each individual case.

4. The credit supply of the formal and informal financial sectors

In the preceding chapters, arguments were presented to explain why banks exclude small and medium-sized enterprises from access to credit. However, this credit rationing in certain market segments becomes a problem only if there are no other institutions which can efficiently serve these market segments. To ascertain whether such institutions are in fact lacking, the supply function of informal lenders is presented and then compared with the credit supply provided by banks, following which the results of the comparison are analysed to determine the implications for the credit market as a whole.

Informal lenders are not part of the formal financial system, and thus are unable to fund their lending activities on relatively attractive terms using credit facilities provided by the central bank and/or savings collected from the general public. Because they operate as disparate entities rather than as an integrated system, it is difficult for them to deal with liquidity mismatches; as a result, their liquidity management is inefficient and therefore costly. For these reasons, they must factor in very high funding costs when setting their prices.

However, they have an advantage over conventional banks – namely, that they can assess the situation of "their" small borrowers with great precision, and thus are not confronted with the problem of asymmetric information. Moreover, they are regarded as belonging to the same social environment as their customers, which significantly increases the borrowers' intrinsic motivation to repay their loans. Although informal lenders are exposed to credit risk if a borrower becomes incapable of repaying his or her loan, they are able to assess this risk relatively well and thus pass on the resulting costs to their customers. Thus, credit risk assessment is not considered a problem, but is instead part of the business. In addition, their transaction costs are relatively low in comparison with those of conventional banks.

In Figure 10, these points have been incorporated into the graph which was elaborated in the preceding chapters. The risk costs (c^{risk}) can be assessed by informal lenders and are independent of the size of the enterprise; these are added to the costs of funds, i_{inf}^{fund}, which are already relatively high. By then adding the transaction costs, which, as in the formal sector, are proportionally higher for very small credits than for "larger" loans, one arrives at the total cost curve for informal lenders which, as an analogue to the cost curve of the banks, represents the minimum interest rates which moneylenders would charge given a particular loan amount or size of enterprise.

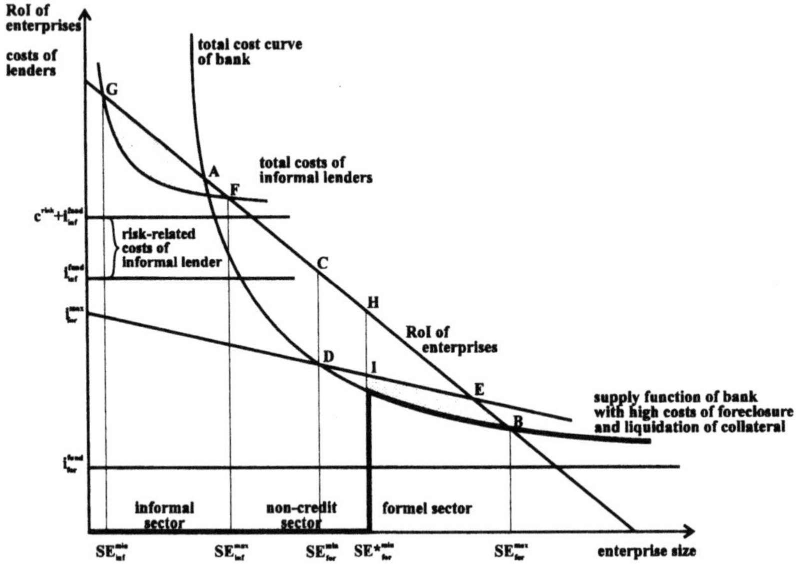

Fig. 10: The credit supply functions of the formal and informal financial sectors

In this graph as well, there is a contract area which lies between the cost curve of the lenders and the RoI of the enterprises, and which defines the range of possible interest rates in the informal credit market. It is apparent that all enterprises of a size between SE_{inf}^{min} and SE_{inf}^{max} will have access to informal credit. In contrast to the formal credit market, credit rationing in the informal market does not occur on the basis of the size of enterprises; however, borrowing simply does not make economic sense for enterprises which are smaller than SE_{inf}^{min} or larger than SE_{inf}^{max}, as they would have to pay interest rates which are higher than their potential RoI.

Conclusions

The implications of the various phenomena outlined above for the credit market as a whole are as follows: relatively small enterprises whose size ranges between SE_{inf}^{min} and SE_{inf}^{max} can obtain financing in the informal credit market (at comparatively high interest rates), while larger enterprises can turn to the formal financial market to procure capital at low interest rates.

The high interest rates prevailing in the informal sector may merely reflect the high cost of small loans. In the example shown in Figure 10, informal lenders actually have competitive advantages over the formal sector at nearly all points on this segment (with the exception of AF). However, this does not have to be the case; if the banks' transaction costs were slightly lower, for example, their total costs curve would shift toward the origin.

The most important finding is that enterprises of a size between SE_{inf}^{max} and $SE^{*}{}_{for}^{min}$[22] can borrow in neither of the two markets. They are too small – and thus unattractive – for formal-sector banks, and the interest rates in the informal sector would be higher than their RoI, i.e. borrowing would be irrational in economic terms. Medium-sized enterprises thus have no access to either formal- or informal-sector financing, which probably has a sustained negative effect on their competitiveness.

22 If the costs of foreclosure and liquidation are relatively low, and $SE^{*}{}_{for}^{min}$ is thus smaller than SE_{for}^{min}, then $SE^{*}{}_{for}^{min}$ must be substituted with SE_{for}^{min} in the text.

Part II. The Impacts of Credit Market Segmentation

In Part I, we determined the causes of credit market segmentation. We shall now examine the impacts of segmentation. Part II begins by analysing the anticipated development of the size distribution of enterprises within a typical economy in order to show, in Chapter 2, that credit market segmentation also gives rise to labour market segmentation. Chapter 3 discusses the efficiency losses at the macro level which result from segmented factor markets, and in Chapter 4 the impact on income distribution is discussed – an aspect which, unfortunately, is often neglected in economic analyses. Chapter 5 examines the stability of factor market segmentation from the perspective of the political economy. Part II concludes by drawing on the findings presented in Parts I and II of this study to explain why the financial sectors of many "developing countries" have tended to evolve according to certain patterns.

1. Size distribution of enterprises in an economy

The preceding analysis showed that, in an environment defined by the set of parameters assumed here, medium-sized enterprises will not have access to credit. If enterprises of this size nonetheless exist, they will necessarily rely on self-financing. It is conceivable that, under constantly changing conditions, these businesses will eventually succeed in evolving into large enterprises. However, their lack of access to credit places them at a competitive disadvantage, and it is thus more likely that they will either have to cease operating at some point or gradually contract until they are no longer medium-sized businesses, dropping into the category of "small enterprises". Given their lack of access to external financing, it is quite difficult for existing medium-sized enterprises to successfully maintain their business operations as long as they remain this size.

Very few new medium-sized enterprises will be established. The preceding analysis revealed that small enterprises have no incentive to attempt to finance their growth through borrowing. At the same time, however, they cannot be expected to achieve growth using internally-generated funds. Although small enterprises usually earn profits significantly in excess of what their operators need for subsistence, these profits are just barely sufficient to meet "additional" expenses for vital needs such as education for the children, a healthy living environment, visits to the doctor, or medicines. Normally, a high priority is given to satisfying these needs, and thus, only a few small entrepreneurs are able to expand their businesses using own funds – namely those who have a lower rate of time preference, e.g. because their children have already grown up and are earning their own income. One can therefore assume that given the market conditions assumed in Part I, very few small enterprises will expand into the medium-sized range.

It is also unlikely that shrinking large enterprises will be able to operate as medium-sized businesses for very long. On the basis of the model, we can conclude that once an enterprise has contracted beyond a certain point, the banks will no longer be interested in catering for its financing needs, with the lack of access to formal-sector loans causing it to lose a competitive advantage. However, we should not assume that this logical implication of the model amounts to a kind of "iron law". Indeed, a "downsized" former large enterprise that has moved into the medium size range has the advantage of being a long-standing customer of its bank, and long-term relationships alleviate the problems of asymmetric information. The maximum interest rate line for this enterprise would shift upward, and it would continue to be able to access credit, although at somewhat higher interest rates.

In many cases, however, contraction indicates that an enterprise's operations are inefficient, or that market conditions exist which are unfavourable for the enterprise. In the model, these factors cause the enterprise's RoI function to shift downward. If, in addition, the enterprise's costs rise, it will have trouble maintaining its position in the market. Medium-sized enterprises are thus often in an intermediate stage on their way toward bankruptcy. Such an enterprise will continue to earn a satisfactory return only in exceptional cases, i.e. when it has no serious competition in its contracting market segment and does not have to contend with price wars.

On the whole, only a few medium-sized enterprises will survive. In other words, businesses of this size are underrepresented in the enterprise sector. Instead, there are mainly small or very small enterprises (in the following, these will be referred to as "small enterprises"), and large or very large enterprises ("large enterprises"). Thus, over the medium term, segmentation in the credit market also gives rise to a segmented size distribution of enterprises. As a result, enterprises are restricted in their development, which is a particularly serious drawback as this lack of dynamism prevents them from adapting to changing external conditions. Moreover, segmented size distribution also prevents the development of a broader-based innovative entrepreneurial class. Because there are so few local entrepreneurs, new large enterprises will most likely be established by foreigners or multinational corporations.

Now that these effects have been derived theoretically, we shall endeavour to verify them empirically. Table 1 shows the distribution of employees among production enterprises of various sizes (small, medium and large) for 14 "developing countries":[23]

Country (Date of study)		Number of employees	
	Small enterprises (<10 employees)	Medium-sized enterprises (10-49 employees)	Large enterprises (≥50 employees)
India (1971)	42%	20%	38%
Tanzania (1967)	56%	7%	37%
Ghana (1970)	84%	1%	15%
Kenya (1969)	49%	10%	41%
Sierra Leone (1974)	90%	5%	5%
Indonesia (1977)	77%	7%	16%
Zambia (1985)	83%	1%	16%
Honduras (1979)	68%	8%	24%
Thailand (1978)	58%	11%	31%
Philippines (1974)	66%	5%	29%
Nigeria (1972)	59%	26%	15%
Jamaica (1978)	35%	16%	49%
Columbia (1973)	52%	13%	35%
Korea (1975)	40%	7%	53%

Tab. 1: The distribution of employees in production enterprises
Source: LIEDHOLM/MEAD, 1987, p. 15.

In all of these countries, with the exception of India and Nigeria, medium-sized enterprises employ less than one sixth of all workers. India is an exception because it has an extremely efficient informal financial market (at least in the cities) which charges interest rates only slightly higher than those offered by banks (2-4% p.a.).[24] The fact that medium-sized businesses account for a

[23] Here, the number of employees is taken as a measure of the size of enterprises, as there are no statistics available on the distribution of employees among enterprises grouped in size categories based on total assets. It can be assumed, however, that the number of employees is a sufficiently accurate proxy here, and thus that the above data are roughly in line with those that would be obtained using total assets.

[24] Cf. TIMBERG/AIYAR, 1984, p. 57

relatively large share of total employment in the production sector in Nigeria is probably a reflection of the important role played by oil exports in that country's economy. Thus, overall, the data provide impressive evidence to support the hypothesis that segmented credit markets lead to a segmented size distribution of enterprises.

Critics could object that these data merely prove the existence of size distribution segmentation with respect to production enterprises. Unfortunately, comprehensive data covering all sectors of relevant economies are not available. However, there are studies which investigate the distribution of workers among all small and medium-sized enterprises, and compare the resulting figures with data on the total population of working age.[25] LIEDHOLM and MEAD speak of the "missing middle. [...] employment is concentrated in microenterprises (10 or less workers) or in very large enterprises (50 or more workers), with few in the 10-50-person range. This phenomenon [...] raises questions as to whether policy or institutional constraints are hindering a process of evolution whereby the smallest enterprises grow into this middle category."[26] Our analysis has shown that even competitive markets can effectively prevent small enterprises from expanding into medium-sized businesses.

2. Labour market segmentation

Thus far, we have demonstrated that only small and large enterprises can exist given the conditions assumed above – i.e. that there will only be an insignificant number of medium-sized businesses in such a setting. Small enterprises finance a portion of their "total assets" by taking out informal loans at very high interest rates. If they are to be able to afford these loans, such enterprises must achieve a very high RoI; this in turn forces them to employ relatively labour-intensive production methods, and thus their labour productivity remains low. Consequently, wage levels are also low.

By contrast, large enterprises can finance their operations quite inexpensively. Accordingly, their operations are capital-intensive, which leads to high labour productivity and high wages.

Thus, the labour market is divided into two segments. Employees of large enterprises earn relatively high wages, whereas wages are low at small businesses. This is not an outgrowth of official restrictions or requirements, but rather a result of market processes taking place under perfect competition! A

---

25 Cf. e.g. LIEDHOLM/MEAD, 1993, p. 11-14, and LIEDHOLM/MEAD, 1998, p. 1-15.

26 LIEDHOLM/MEAD, 1993, p.12.

segmented credit market thus gives rise to segmentation not only of the size distribution of enterprises, but of labour markets as well.

Small enterprises usually operate in the informal sector. On the one hand, this is because excessive official requirements relating to the registration of businesses and bureaucratic impediments make it relatively expensive for them to become formal enterprises. However, becoming part of the formal sector also has advantages, e.g. formal businesses enjoy the protection of the legal system and have recourse to the courts to enforce claims. Nonetheless, the costs of formalisation are not closely correlated to the size of the enterprise, whereas the advantages of formalisation do increase in proportion to its size. Thus, there is a "critical enterprise size" with respect to formalisation. For all enterprises which exceed this size, it makes economic sense to become part of the formal sector.

The inability or unwillingness of small enterprises to formalise their operations is thus also attributable to the growth constraints they face, which, as demonstrated above, are a result of credit market segmentation. Whenever this critical enterprise size is larger than the "maximum size for small enterprises" as determined by the credit market, formalisation will be economically disadvantageous for such small enterprises, and it will therefore be difficult to induce them to join the formal sector.

Thus, a large informal sector exists – or arises in the first place – owing to the effects of bureaucratic obstacles to formalisation in combination with credit market segmentation.

Figure 11 illustrates the segmentation of credit and labour markets as depicted by the Heckscher-Ohlin model.[27] In contrast to the conventional representations, this model employs not two, but three sectors in order to describe more accurately the complex reality of these markets. In industrial sector 1 (I1), "tradable good 1" is manufactured using a linear-limitational production process.[28] I1 is the unit-value isoquant which represents the various factor combinations that would enable good 1 to be produced in a quantity which has a value of US$ 1.

---

27 For a description of the basic HECKSCHER-OHLIN model, cf. ROSE, 1989, pp. 314-317. An obvious disadvantage of this model is that it abstracts from transaction and information costs; in the line of reasoning presented here so far, however, the existence of these costs constituted the basis for deriving segmentation in the first place. Nonetheless, the model can be used to illustrate certain fundamental effects of segmentation, although this logical inconsistency necessarily makes the model less precise.

28 Limitationality is not a central assumption, but rather an approximation of reality. There would be no qualitative change in the correlations derived below if the elasticity of factor substitution were greater.

Analogously, isoquant I2 describes the possible combinations that could be used in the production of good 2, with a moderate factor substitution elasticity being assumed. In the third sector, isoquant NT plots the possible combinations that could be used in the production of non-tradable goods.

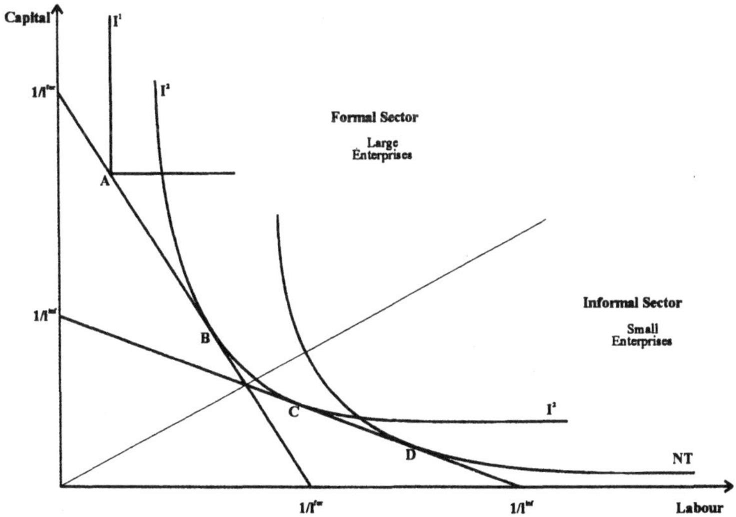

Fig. 11: Segmented factor markets as explained by the Heckscher-Ohlin model

In competitive markets, prices of factors and goods emerge at which enterprises can produce and sell their goods and services without incurring losses, but also without earning significant profits. This implies that entrepreneurs merely earn "profits" in the form of the return on the capital they employ plus an amount which compensates them for their tangible, measurable labour input. This assumption is not particularly realistic, above all in "developing countries", where entrepreneurship is a very scarce factor and those who can provide this "input" are compensated very generously for doing so.

Nonetheless, this model is very useful for further analysis if it is assumed that the entrepreneurs' compensation has already been integrated into the isoquants. For example, isoquant I^1 could represent a quantity of goods worth US$ 1.20 from which a profit margin of US$ 0.20 has already been deducted and which serves as remuneration for the extremely scarce factor "entrepreneurship". Because entrepreneurs will become active in those areas in which they can achieve particularly high profits, one can also assume that, as is the case with other factors, their "factor payment" is identical in the various sectors among which they can choose when deciding where to operate. To simplify matters, this constant can therefore be ignored in the analysis. Accordingly, in the following discussion it is assumed that the isoquants have already been adjusted to account for the entrepreneurs' profits, and thus for the remainder of this chapter it can also be assumed that entrepreneurs cannot earn exceptionally high profits, i.e. that perfect competition exists.

The auxiliary assumption of perfect competition makes it easier to depict the static effects of factor market segmentation. When the dynamic effects are investigated in the next chapter, this auxiliary assumption will be dispensed with.

Under perfect competition, the price ratios must be such that the factor price lines – i.e. the factor combinations which result in costs of US$ 1 – are tangent to the isoquants. Given the positions of the isoquants in the diagram, there is not a single line which would fulfil this condition. This is not surprising, for we have already seen that factor prices must be different for small and large enterprises.

The segmentation of the credit and labour markets is shown in Figure 11. Here, the line running through points A and B represents factor prices for large enterprises, i.e. enterprises with high wage levels and low capital costs, while the line running through points C and D represents factor prices for small enterprises. Because the cost of capital is high for small enterprises, their operations are relatively labour intensive. This explains, on the one hand, why they are the sole suppliers in the labour-intensive non-tradable goods sector and, on the other, why they produce industrial good 2, which is also manufactured by large enterprises, using a comparatively labour-intensive technology (point C).

The operations of large enterprises are capital intensive, they are the only suppliers in capital-intensive sector 1. They are also active in sector 2 alongside the informal small enterprises; however, even in this sector their operations are relatively capital intensive (point B). The term "capital intensive" is used to contrast their mode of production with that of small enterprises within the same economy, not with ways of producing goods that are typically employed in other economies. It is quite possible that the type of production we are discussing here, which is relatively capital intensive by the standards of the local economy, would turn out to be labour intensive in comparison with production in other countries.

The division of factor markets into two competitive segments that function independently of each other is illustrated with particular clarity by the factor box

(Stolper-Samuelson theorem).[29] Figure 12 divides up the entire available factor stock in an economy between the formal and informal sectors. The formal sector, i.e. large enterprises, has a stock of labour and capital corresponding to the factor box which covers the area between 0for and point C. Correspondingly, the informal sector works with the factors in the box between point C and 0inf.

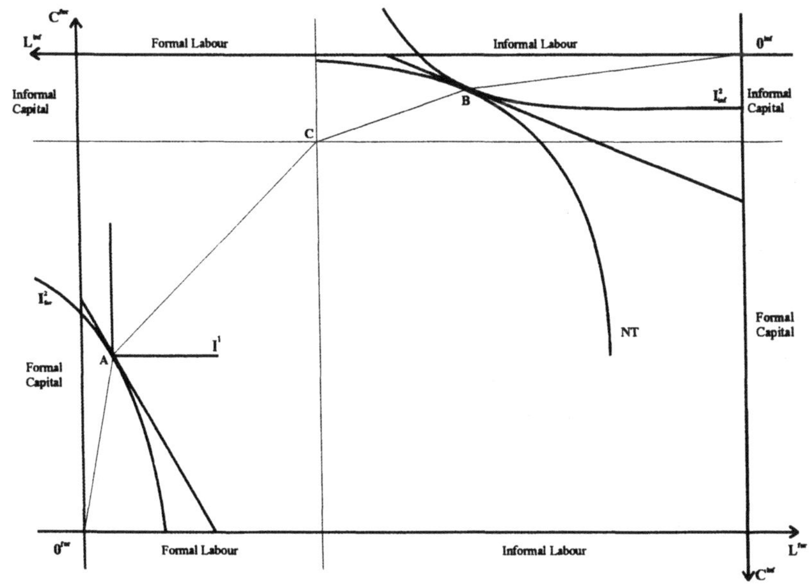

Fig. 12: Segmentation of factor markets: the factor box

One can see that the formal sector has a comparatively large supply of capital. It uses the factors 0for - A to produce I1, and A - C to produce I2. Point A is a point of tangency for both isoquants, and it is also where factor prices are determined. If the markets are functioning, the factor price line must also be tangent to both isoquants. The relatively steep slope of the line at point A indicates that wages are relatively high and interest rates are relatively low.

Conversely, the informal sector has relatively little capital. It uses the factors which correspond to segment CB to produce I^2, and the remaining factors (B - 0^{inf}) to produce non-tradable goods and services. The informal sector is also a functioning market segment, i.e. its factors are fully employed and they are

---

29 For information on the basic model of the STOLPER-SAMUELSON theorem, cf. STOLPER/SAMUIELSON,1941.

remunerated in line with their marginal value product. This is illustrated by point B, a point of tangency for both isoquants where the factor price line has the same slope as the isoquants. The relatively gentle slope of this line indicates low wages and high interest rates.

The question remains as to how two completely independent market segments can emerge within one economy with very different factor prices and no tendency toward price convergence. Two possible ways of resolving this problem must be considered: factor prices could converge, on the one hand, through the movement of factors into the specific market segment in which a higher remuneration is offered, or, on the other hand, by the process described in the factor-price equalisation theorem[30] – in other words, via "trade" between the formal and the informal sectors.

As was demonstrated in Part I, capital will not "migrate" into the informal sector. Although the people employed in the informal sector would gladly work in the formal sector, they are unable to do so because there are not enough formal-sector jobs to go round. There are two reasons why wages in the formal sector do not drop dramatically: on the one hand, labour productivity in this sector is high; on the other hand, its workforce is relatively easy to organise. Particularly in cases where production is highly capital-intensive, it is important for entrepreneurs to have employees who are loyal and reliable. The money they would save by paying workers less would not compensate for the loss of stability and continuity in their labour force. Moreover, as a result of the wage differential between the formal and informal sectors, pressure can be brought to bear on workers, for they would have to accept a significant reduction in income if they were fired. Shapiro and Stiglitz showed that it can be completely rational for employers to pay wages which are higher than the "equilibrium wage", because by doing so they can alleviate the problems of asymmetric information between employer and employee.[31] Thus, one cannot expect that there will be "factor mobility" between these two market segments.

The only other possible solution is for factor-price equalisation to occur through "trade". According to the factor-price equalisation theorem, factor prices will necessarily converge as a result of free trade. Within an individual economy, free trade exists by definition because no tariffs are levied. However, the theorem explicitly derives factor-price equalisation only for situations in which countries do not specialise in the production of one good to the exclusion

30 Cf. SAMUELSON, 1948, 1949, 1953-54 and 1967.

31 Cf. SHAPIRO/STIGLITZ, 1984, pp. 433-444; YELLEN, 1984, pp. 200-205; STIGLITZ, 1985, pp. 595-618; and GREENWALD/STIGLITZ, 1987, pp. 444-456.

of the other.[32] In our example, however, only the formal sector is in a position to manufacture product I1, while the informal sector is the sole provider of non-tradable goods. Thus, complete specialisation exists in both sectors, and factor prices will not converge.

Consequently, there are no market forces which could help eliminate or reduce segmentation. Given the assumptions specified above, the segmentation of the factor markets, which results from credit market segmentation, is permanent, i.e. an "equilibrium state". It is especially noteworthy that, despite the assumption of perfect competition, production takes place at two different levels of both labour and capital productivity, and that factor prices differ, but without these differentials causing the factors which command a lower price to "migrate" to other sectors.

3. Efficiency losses at the macro level

In the preceding two chapters, it was shown that credit market segmentation also gives rise to a segmented size distribution of enterprises as well as a segmented labour market. Yet why is this a bad thing? The next two chapters attempt to answer this question. Chapter 3 investigates the efficiency losses which occur at the macro level as a result of the various types of segmentation, while Chapter 4 examines the negative effects of segmentation on income distribution. We will begin by taking a look at the static efficiency losses which can be derived by applying neoclassical theory, in order to then shed light on the dynamic effects, which are probably much more serious.

a) Static efficiency losses as an outgrowth of dualistic structures

Production in an economy can only be efficient if the factors of production are employed fully and in line with their relative scarcity, i.e. if the ratio of their marginal products corresponds to the factor price ratio. On a graph, this condition is met when the isoquants have the same slope as the factor price line at each of the production points.

According to this definition, both the formal and informal sectors work efficiently with the factors available to them. However, this is not the case for the economy as a whole because the factor price lines of the formal and informal sectors have different slopes. Differing factor prices or factor marginal product

32 Cf. ROSE, 1989, pp. 328-330.

ratios suggest that there are inefficiencies at the macro level which we will now examine more closely.

For the sake of clarity, the efficiency losses will be subdivided into four groups: *first-degree efficiency losses* arise when factors are allocated inefficiently within industrial sector I^2. Owing to a lack of factor substitution between the formal and informal portions of this sector, factor input ratios will vary between the two segments, causing output to decline.

However, even if industrial sector I^2 were to use its factors efficiently, under the prevailing conditions *second-degree efficiency losses* would nonetheless occur. These would arise because there would still be a lack of factor substitution between the various sectors, which would in turn cause the marginal productivity of factors to be different for each of the three sectors.

If factors were also used efficiently between the sectors, the increases in efficiency and output would lead to changes in product prices, which could once again cause a shift in the distribution of economic activity among the sectors. Such effects constitute *third-degree efficiency losses.*

Changes in factor and product prices can lead to changes in the factor supply. This not only alters the dimensions of the factor box, and thus production conditions, but also has an influence on the level and distribution of income. Depending on the relevant income elasticities, this in turn impacts the demand for the various products. All of these effects together constitute *fourth-degree efficiency losses*.

The analysis presented in the following will be limited to first- and second-degree efficiency losses, as these are usually of far greater significance than the latter two types of loss. In addition, third- and fourth-degree efficiency losses are a function of so many factors, such as the elasticity of supply and demand in product and factor markets, that a general analysis would go beyond the scope of this work.

First-degree efficiency losses are shown in Figure 13, which is based on the factor-box diagram presented in the preceding chapter. In the first step, the isoquants of the formal and informal segments of industrial sector 2 have additionally been transposed through point C. The same has been done with the two factor price lines, $(l/i)^{for}$ and $(l/i)^{inf}$. It is clear that although the factor price lines are tangent to their respective isoquants, there are nonetheless considerable differences between the formal and informal segments (illustrated by angle α). The area between the two isoquants forms a lens which represents the scope for enhancing efficiency. If both segments of industrial sector 2 were to work with the same factor ratios (determined by the slope of line AB), they could reduce their factor input by a quantity of EL^1 without reducing their output volume. EL^1 thus represents the first-degree efficiency loss.

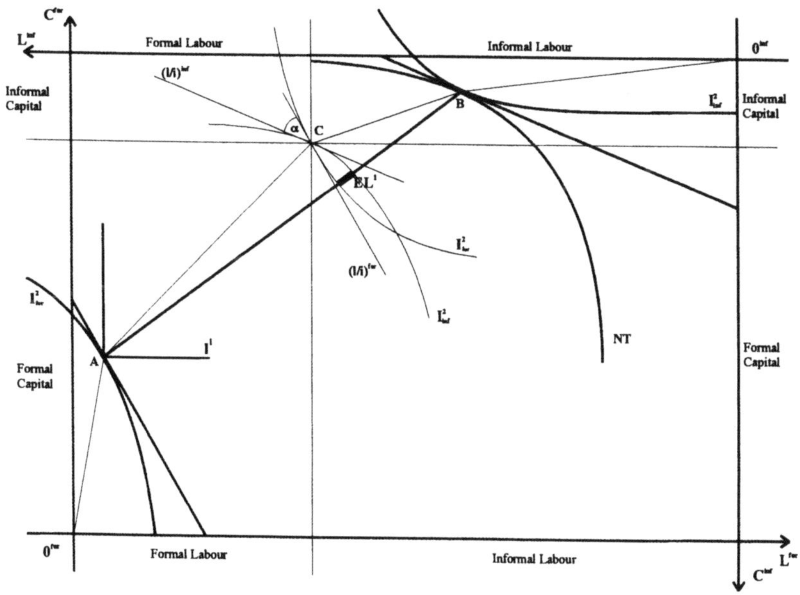

Fig. 13: Factor market segmentation and first-degree efficiency loss

To determine the **second-degree efficiency loss**, it will be assumed that an efficient factor substitution already takes place between the two segments of industrial sector 2, i.e. both segments operate with the same factor input ratio. We will now examine factor substitutions amongst all three sectors which increase efficiency. Of course, the assumption that industrial sector 1 is characterised by a linear-limitational production function also leads to the conclusion that factor substitution is not useful in this case. If the elasticity of factor substitution were greater, the processes derived in the following with respect to factor substitution between industrial sector 2 and the non-tradable goods sector would occur here as well.

In Figure 14, a common isoquant (I^2_{total}) has been plotted for both segments of industrial sector 2, with point A marking the point of origin. This isoquant indicates the factor combinations with which the combined total output of the two segments can be maintained at the previous level. The slope of this isoquant obviously deviates from the slope of the isoquant for non-tradable goods at point

B, and thus in this case as well a lens is formed which represents the scope for enhancing efficiency.

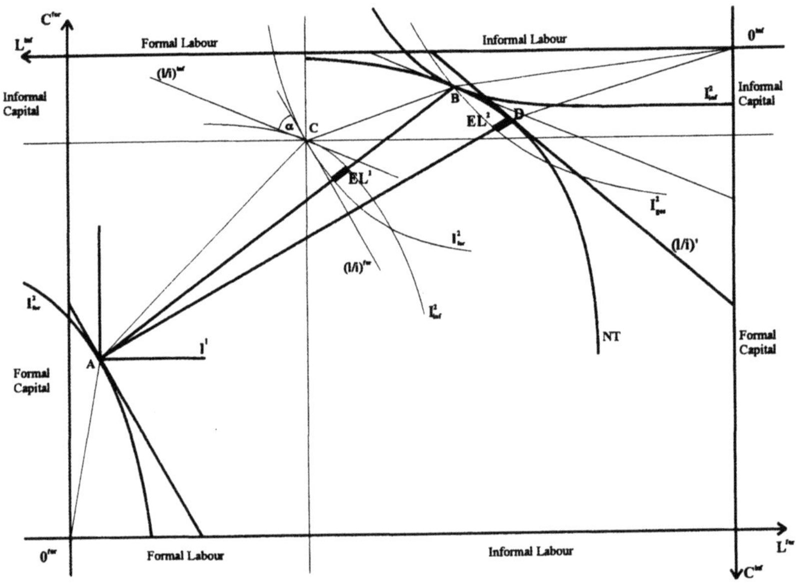

Fig. 14: Factor market segmentation and second-degree efficiency loss

An efficiency-enhancing exchange of factors between the two sectors will create a situation in which the production of non-tradable goods becomes more capital intensive, in keeping with the factor input ratio determined by line $D0^{inf}$. Industrial sector 2 does not require the entire remaining stock of factors (AD) to sustain its prior output level, but instead can reduce its factor input by the quantity EL^2. EL^2 thus represents the second-degree efficiency loss.

The line (l/i)' represents the factor prices which emerge, i.e. higher wages and lower interest rates than in the informal sector $(l/i)^{inf}$, and lower wages and higher interest rates than in the formal sector $(l/i)^{for}$. The new factor price line applies to all segments of the economy, including industrial sector 1. An exchange of factors would thus eliminate segmentation.

A simple solution to a difficult problem? In fact, it is not quite as simple as it seems. On the one hand, in Part I it was shown that a factor exchange in the capital market is highly unlikely; this lack of factor mobility in turn gave rise to the other types of segmentation. Yet even if it were possible to increase the mobility of capital between the sectors significantly, one should not assume that this would lead to uniform factor prices. Indeed, as was mentioned above, the factor-box diagram completely disregards transaction costs and risk-related costs. Lending to large enterprises in industrial sector 1 will always be less expensive than lending to small enterprises which produce non-tradable goods. However, improved factor mobility would make it possible to reduce the extent of price differentiation. Thus, the conclusions which one can draw from Figure 14 are certainly not wrong, but the causal relationships that are highlighted by the diagram are less well defined, and less absolute, in reality that they appear to be here. Therefore, increased factor mobility between the sectors does not fully resolve the static efficiency problems, but rather sets in motion a process of gradual improvement.

b) Dynamic effects of dualistic structures

The dynamic effects of dualistic structures probably have far more serious consequences than the static efficiency losses. As was demonstrated in Chapter 1, credit market segmentation makes it very difficult for medium-sized enterprises to operate successfully. It was shown that small businesses are unlikely to grow, and that large enterprises are unlikely to be able to function at a size smaller than the "formal minimum enterprise size".

Enterprises will sometimes be forced to adapt their size to accommodate changing external conditions. When the market segment of a large enterprise contracts, it is preferable for the enterprise to likewise reduce the scope of its economic activity rather than close down altogether. Smaller "large enterprises" are, so to speak, on the edge of the abyss: there are limits to how far they can decline in size, because if they become too small they will forfeit their access to bank loans.[33] They also risk losing this access if the credit supply provided by the banking sector is reduced, for whatever reason – e.g. due to the adoption of a contractionary monetary policy. If this happens, smaller large enterprises will be the first businesses to find that their source of formal credit has dried up. The inability to obtain loans will drive many of these enterprises to ruin, despite the fact that, otherwise, they are economically sound businesses which would otherwise be able to survive and compete in their respective markets. At the

[33] As mentioned above, long-term borrower-lender relationships diminish the information problem and cause the interest rate ceiling function to shift upwards. This gives former large enterprises a certain degree of leeway in paring down their operations, and even allows them to shrink to a size which is smaller than the "minimum enterprise size" for the formal sector. Nonetheless, there is still a point beyond which they will lose their access to credit if they continue to contract.

same time, this susceptibility to shocks limits the range of options open to national economic policy.

As was demonstrated earlier, credit market segmentation also makes it much more difficult for small enterprises to expand into the medium-sized range. This in turn prevents new, innovative enterprises from emerging which could develop new market niches. It also inhibits the formation of a broad, dynamic entrepreneurial class whose individual members are able to adapt their businesses rapidly and flexibly to changing conditions in their markets and in the overall economic environment.

The existing small entrepreneurs cannot be said to constitute an "entrepreneurial class" because they are scarcely in a position to develop a significant innovation potential owing to legal and bureaucratic obstacles, as well as to their lack of resources. Their "achievement" consists more in simply surviving than in establishing dynamic enterprises that can grow and adapt to changing conditions in the marketplace; moreover, the skills and abilities needed to achieve this outcome do not constitute a scarce resource, and thus – unlike the situation in the formal sector, where, as a scarce "input", genuine entrepreneurship commands a high price – those who possess such skills do not receive any special remuneration. Thus, people who run this type of business should be referred to as "self-employed persons" rather than "entrepreneurs".

The lack of a broad stratum of medium-sized enterprises not only dramatically reduces the innovative potential of an economy. Very large enterprises often react too late to changes in external conditions; on the other hand, "smaller " large enterprises can only respond within certain, narrow limits, as we have shown above. This impaired ability to adapt causes the system as a whole to be more susceptible to shocks. Moreover, entrepreneurship commands a very high price because it is such a scarce factor. However, as the local economy produces scarcely any "home-grown" entrepreneurs, the generous remuneration of entrepreneurial inputs attracts foreign entrepreneurs who provide these inputs and then, as a rule, transfer the large profits abroad which can made through entrepreneurial activity. The economy comes to depend on foreign entrepreneurs, which in turn increases its susceptibility to shocks in the form of capital flight.

4. Consequences for income distribution

This chapter examines the consequences of segmented factor markets for income distribution. We will begin by taking a look at functional income distribution, considering the formal and informal sectors separately. This will then enable us to arrive at conclusions concerning personal income distribution.

a) Functional income distribution

A detailed overview of the functional distribution of income is provided below. Adjectives such as "high" or "very low" always indicate a comparison with the income levels that would emerge in the same economy if its factor markets were not segmented (and had not been segmented for a relatively long period of time). In addition to investment income and earned income (remuneration of labour), the (additional) income obtained as remuneration for entrepreneurial activity has also been taken into account.

	Formal sector	Informal sector
Earned income	relatively high	very low
Investment income	very low	very high
Income from entre-preneurial activity	very high	very low

Tab. 2: Functional income distribution given segmented factor markets

As was already mentioned in the preceding chapters, the cost of capital – and thus investment income – is very low in the formal sector. In the past, particularly during the era of "financial repression", real interest rates in many countries were negative, as was formal-sector "investment income", which thus became a cost factor. As a result, wages in this sector were – and, as was shown above, still are – relatively high. Because entrepreneurial activity is a scarce factor, it also commands a very high price.

In many respects, the informal sector is the mirror image of the formal sector. Capital is very expensive, and consequently wages are very low. There is little entrepreneurial activity as defined by Schumpeter. Indeed, the main achievement of "micro entrepreneurs" is to survive; they are much less likely to build up dynamic entrepreneurial institutions which can grow and adapt to changing conditions in the marketplace. Consequently, the income of these micro entrepreneurs consists mainly of their RoI plus the remuneration they receive for their labour input. In the informal sector, very little income is derived from entrepreneurial activity.

b) Personal income distribution

The findings with respect to functional income distribution will now be used as the basis for an assessment of personal income distribution. To this end, we will attempt to determine which social groups receive each of the various types of income. For the sake of simplicity, the following analysis will be limited to three "groups": the "rich", the "well-off" and the "poor" (see the overview presented in Table 3). These ideal-typical groups have been used exclusively for the purpose of structuring the analysis, and the designations employed here should not be misunderstood as having ideological connotations associated with the notion of class struggle.

	Earned income	Investment income	Cost of credit	Income from entrepreneurial activity
"The rich"	Insignificant for entrepreneurs; very high for persons in senior positions	Capital is invested primarily abroad	Very low or negative for formal enterprise loans	Very high, as entrepreneurship is an extremely scarce factor
"The well-off"	Relatively high for typical kinds of employment in the formal sector	Small balances in accounts in the formal sector for the purpose of liquidity management; the investment income level for informal moneylenders is high	Low costs for mortgages or consumer loans	Formal-sector workers are not active as entrepreneurs; informal moneylenders may be able to skim off monopoly rents
"The poor"	Very low	Savings deposits in the formal sector earn very low or negative interest	Informal enterprise loans are very expensive	Very low, because they are not entrepreneurs as defined by Schumpeter

Tab. 3: Personal income distribution given segmented factor markets

The *rich* work either as entrepreneurs or as high-level employees in the formal sector. The latter earn very high incomes for the work they perform, while the former are mainly remunerated for their input as entrepreneurs. Investment income need not be taken into account in this analysis, as most surplus funds are either invested in real estate or channelled into investments abroad. In addition, entrepreneurs need equity capital to implement their projects and to qualify for bank loans. However, the low return on the capital they invest in their businesses is more than compensated by a) the very low or negative real interest rates on the bank loans which they can take out to finance their operations, and b) the fact that entrepreneurship is very well-compensated. Overall, the volume of real estate loans and enterprise loans which the banking sector disburses to this group tends to be larger than the volume of savings deposits it holds at formal banks. Thus, its members are net borrowers and profit from the low interest rates. Moreover, segmentation effectively protects them against strong competition, which they would inevitably have to face if a broad entrepreneurial class were to develop, and the formation of such a class would clearly be feasible in the absence of segmentation.

The *well-off* are the "middle class", which comprises the hourly-paid and salaried workers of the formal sector on the one hand, and informal moneylenders on the other. As shown above, formal-sector employees earn relatively high wages. They have little if any investment income because the balances they maintain in bank accounts are used mainly as a liquidity reserve. Because of their stable employment situation, they often qualify for consumer loans or even small mortgages in the formal financial sector, which means that they too are net borrowers and, like the rich, benefit from the low interest rates.

Informal moneylenders receive their income from the provision of loans to informal small and micro enterprises. They will be successful only if they can assess their customers' situation with relative accuracy. On the one hand, having to procure the information needed to make such an assessment limits their activities to a comparatively small group of borrowers; at the same time, however, it also serves as a market entry barrier for potential competitors, enabling moneylenders to skim off monopoly rents. Owing to factor market segmentation, the income level of informal lenders is relatively high; at the same time, however, their credit technology prevents them from increasing their income beyond this level.

The *poor* work in the informal sector, and most of the members of this group are self-employed or work in family businesses. They receive very little income. They usually hold savings deposits at banks as a reserve for emergencies. Because they seldom qualify for bank loans, they are net savers in the formal financial system and thus are affected adversely by the low or negative real interest rates. They must obtain part of the capital they require through expensive informal credits,[34] which not only further reduces their income, but also rules out any chance of sustained growth in their businesses (see above). Although they are self-employed, they can hardly be described as entrepreneurs in the true sense of the word, and thus, at best, they receive only a very small additional amount of compensation for the activities they carry out as operators of businesses.

Factor market segmentation therefore places people who are already poor at an even greater disadvantage. On the one hand, their income level is reduced still further; on the other, they are largely prevented from increasing their incomes, e.g. by expanding their businesses. By contrast, the rich can enhance their income and are protected from additional competition. The well-off also profit from the situation, and while they do not derive great benefits from segmentation, they nonetheless gain enough from it to lead comparatively comfortable lives with relatively certain prospects for the future. Factor market segmentation thus exacerbates existing differences in income, leads to increased income concentration, and makes income distribution in the economy less equitable.

5. The stability of the system

Chapter 3 of Part II showed that segmented factor markets result in static output losses as well as a sustained reduction in overall economic growth. In addition, the preceding chapter demonstrated that factor market segmentation causes income to be distributed less evenly within a society. Thus, two goals which are usually incompatible – namely, equitable income distribution and growth — are rendered complementary, and one would expect that in all countries, economic policymakers would do their utmost to reduce the extent of segmentation and promote informal micro enterprises.

---

34 The fact that poor people deposit their savings at banks where they receive hardly any interest, and at the same time take out expensive loans from informal moneylenders, might seem irrational. In fact, the interest rate differential can be seen as a kind of insurance premium: In an emergency, borrowers can refuse to make loan instalments, or postpone payments, *and simultaneously* draw on their savings. If their savings had been used to repay part of the loan, or if they had used their savings in place of a loan and not borrowed in the first place, they would have been forced to take out an additional loan quickly to deal with the emergency. As poor people have no guarantee that they will have access to credit when they need it, this alternative solution to the "insurance problem" – namely, borrowing - which would be much cheaper, is not an option for the members of this group. Cf. MOMMARTZ/SCHMIDT, 1996, App. B4a) pp. 3-5.

In fact, many governments have taken up the cause of promoting the informal sector. Yet the practical impact of the official policy commitments is usually undermined by a striking lack of concrete action in this area. Take, for example, the situation in El Salvador: "Of course, as everywhere, official policy declarations in El Salvador often recognise, and praise, the role of microenterprises. But facts speak louder than words. [...] the fact that a government commission on the development of the microenterprise sector which was composed of high-ranking officials did not even hold a single working session serves to underscore the validity of the general complaint about government neglect of this sector."[35]

How can one explain this refusal to reduce segmentation through the targeted promotion of the informal sector? After all, implementation of such a policy would simultaneously make income distribution less skewed and foster growth.

This question can only be answered if one applies politico-economic theory: what is beneficial for a society as a whole will by no means be favourable for all strata within that society.[36] The "rich" tend to control the levers of political and economic power. As described above, they profit from the existing segmentation and thus have no interest in changing the status quo. If they are to be forced to change their policies through political pressure, those affected must be able to organise themselves into groups that can bring such pressure to bear in an effective manner. The wage- and salary-earners in the formal sector would be in the best position to do this, yet they also profit from the existing situation. In fact, increases in formal-sector incomes only serve to exacerbate the problem of factor market segmentation.

By contrast, the poor people who work in the informal sector constitute a group which is much too heterogeneous to form a "united front" even over the medium term. They are far too preoccupied with eking out an existence to be able to afford the "luxury" of becoming politically active. If their situation becomes so desperate that even their very survival is in jeopardy, they may well resolve to take collective action over the short term. However, protests of this kind can easily be neutralised with the most rudimentary forms of emergency aid and a few essentially meaningless commitments to improve conditions (see above). Because the poor are unable to organise themselves on anything like a sustainable basis, those who make such commitments cannot be forced to deliver on their promises. The poor are inevitably frustrated by this "failure of politics" and by the perceived ineffectiveness of political action, which further

---

35 MOMMARTZ/SCHMIDT, 1996, p. 17.

36 For a discussion of "political economics", cf. OLSON, 1968.

impedes their ability to organise themselves effectively to protect their interests. The system of segmented factor markets is thus stable in politico-economic terms.

Explaining historical patterns of financial market development

The theoretical results derived thus far will now be used to explain historical patterns of market development in many countries. At the same time, it will be demonstrated that the problem of segmentation cannot be resolved merely by eliminating the factors which led to its emergence.

Until well into the 1980s, governments and development co-operation agencies attempted to promote growth in smallholder agriculture and in the small and micro enterprise sector – and, by so doing, to boost incomes in both of these segments of the economy – by providing them with subsidised loans. At the same time, it was hoped that this policy would cause the informal credit sector, which was regarded as being usurious, to dry up. Regulations were passed which obliged the banks to meet quotas by channelling certain shares of their total lending volume to favoured groups of borrowers, often at negative real interest rates. Maintenance of the intended target-group orientation was to be guaranteed by placing limits on the size of loans.[37]

The subsidy components of these programmes were sizeable: in Costa Rica, for example, 30% of the loan amount was subsidised; in Brazil, subsidies were equivalent to between US$ 3 billion and US$ 4 billion annually.[38] These subsidies were paid for in part with funds provided by development co-operation institutions and in part by expanding the money supply, which in turn fuelled inflation. In such a situation, poor people are disproportionately affected by the resulting "inflation tax" because, on the one hand, they tend to hold a higher share of their assets in the form of currency and, on the other, due to the relatively small amounts involved, they find it difficult or impossible to avoid paying this "tax".[39]

Of course, the subsidies were also attractive to the rich. In fact, it was revealed that "the capacity of such borrowers [*large-scale borrowers, author's*

---

37 Cf. e.g. ADAMS/GRAHAM, 1981, p. 349.

38 Cf. VOGEL, 1984, p. 135f; and ADAMS/GRAHAM, 1981, pp. 352-359. These figures are quite typical. In 1994, as part of a bilateral programme to promote ethnic Germans in Russia, loans were still being granted with a subsidy component equivalent to over 60% (!) of the loan amount.

39 For a discussion of the inflation tax as an economic concept, see GILLIS et al, 1987, pp. 334-336.

note] to manipulate any institution, and the price of its credit, to their own advantage"[40] was such that they were able to neutralise any control mechanisms which governments were able to devise.[41] Thus, VOGEL shows that in Costa Rica 55% of the total volume of "small loans" went to a small group representing only 1.2% of the borrowers.[42] In a 1981 study of bilateral programmes being implemented in the framework of German development co-operation activities in Nicaragua, Colombia and Ecuador, NITSCH/SCHMIDT/-ZEITINGER even proved that not a single small loan went to the poor. Instead, all funds ended up in the pockets of a few rich people.[43]

The effect of this policy was that although bank loans carried very low – as a rule, even negative – real interest rates, they were available to only a few of the banks' large-scale customers.

This situation will now be explained in terms of the basic model presented in Part I. Figure 15 shows a set of possible market conditions prior to the start of the programmes. The banks have cost structures which are a function of the size of the loans granted or of the size of their customers' enterprises; thus, interest rates on bank loans vary. Because the banks have established long-term relationships with their customers, they can assess credit risks relatively well. There is little reason for them to fear moral hazard, as their customers rely on these long-term credit relationships.

In comparison with the banks, informal lenders have higher funding costs but lower transaction costs. In our example, enterprises of all sizes have access to at least one type of credit, and enterprises whose size is between A and F can even choose between formal and informal loans. One could also imagine other situations in which enterprises of a certain size have no access to credit. However, the important thing is that this size range is relatively small because credit relationships are well-established and have existed for a long time, which also makes it feasible for the banks to grant relatively small loans.

---

40 LIPTON, 1984, p 134.

41 Moreover, it is questionable to what extent the governments truly backed their own official programmes. After all, they were made up mostly of people from the same social stratum as the large borrowers who in the end reaped the benefits of the programmes.

42 Cf. VOGEL, 1984, p. 136.

43 Cf. NITSCH/SCHMIDT/ZEITINGER, 1981.

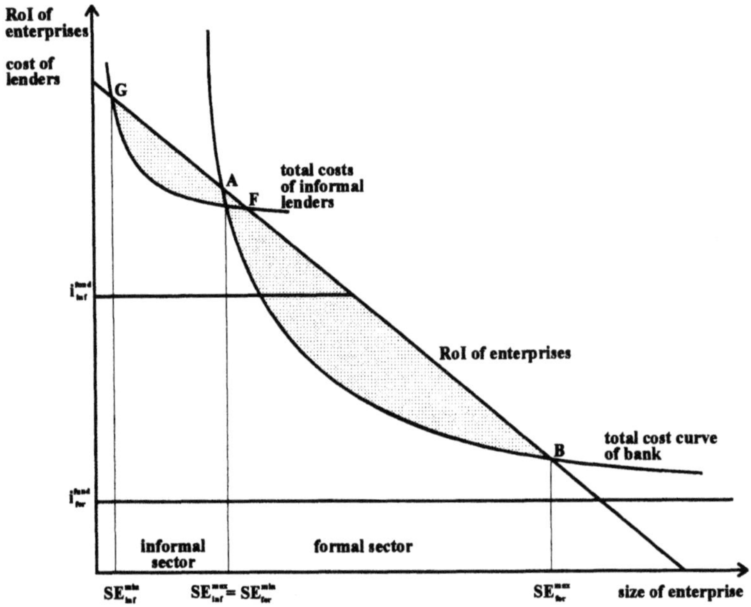

Fig. 15: The credit market prior to the introduction of subsidised credit programmes

Figure 16, which is analogous to Figure 3, depicts, in simplified form, the effects of credit programmes which are based on statutory interest rate ceilings. The figure abstracts from reality in so far as it does not reflect the fact that the exclusion of medium-sized enterprises from access to credit would affect the banks' cost of funds, and specifically that this exclusion causes their cost of funds to drop.[44] This simplification is justifiable because, if it were not made, the outcome would not be qualitatively different, and in quantitative terms the effects would merely be amplified.

As was argued in Part I, if the banks must comply with statutory interest rate ceilings, it no longer makes economic sense for them to lend to medium-sized companies. While interest rate regulations are difficult to circumvent effectively, it is easier to get around government requirements with respect to favoured groups of borrowers or limitations on the size of loans. As a result, if statutory interest rate ceilings are in effect, banks will be willing to lend only to enterprises which demand large loans. The subsidisation of credit will produce the same effect.

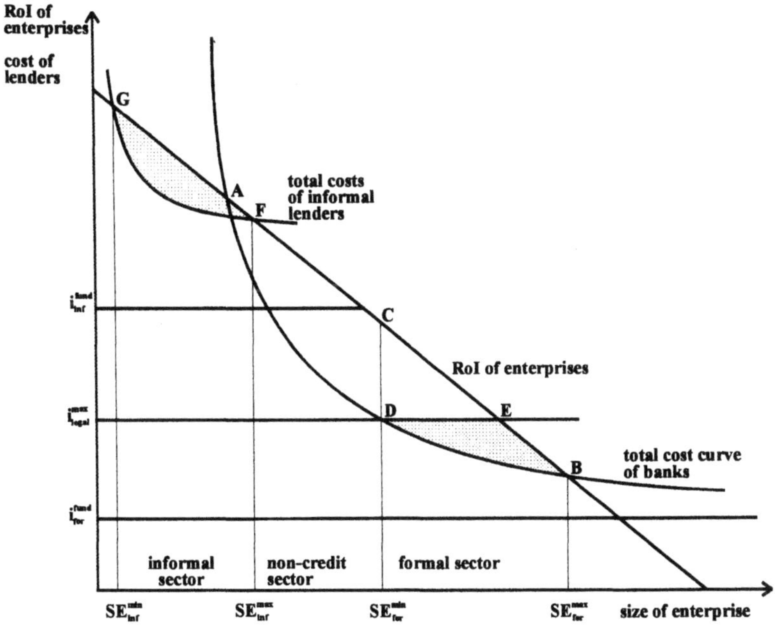

Fig. 16: The impacts of interest rate ceilings on enterprise loans

From this point on, the assumption that medium-sized enterprises have permanently lost their access to bank loans is important for our analysis: long-term credit relationships cease to exist, and as a result, medium-sized businesses become increasingly rare until finally there are hardly any businesses of this size left (see the argument presented in Chapter 1 of Part II). Thus, it can be demonstrated that in practice the policy of subsidising credit did not have the intended effect of improving the situation of small and medium-sized enterprises. Instead, it caused the credit markets to become even more segmented, or gave rise to segmentation where none had existed previously.

Responding to pressure brought to bear on them by the Bretton Woods institutions, the governments of most countries have in the meantime abandoned this policy of requiring banks to grant loans at low interest rates to politically favoured target groups. Interest rate ceilings have been abolished altogether or set so high that they have lost their binding character. Nonetheless, the factor markets are still segmented, and hardly any loans are granted to small and medium-sized enterprises.

44 Cf. TSCHACH, 1995, pp. 4-10.

The explanation for this instance of market failure is provided by Figure 17, which depicts a situation analogous to the one described in Part I: the banks are now confronted with an implicit interest rate ceiling function (i^{max}_{for}) because they must contend with more serious information problems stemming from the fact that they no longer "know" potential borrowers in the medium-sized enterprise category on the basis of long-term business relationships. As a result, the portion of the market in which the banks can operate profitably is no longer as large as it was prior to the introduction of subsidised loans, when it comprised enterprises of a size range extending from A to B. Now, the profitable segment extends only from C' to B. In other words, the profitable area of the market can be enlarged, but not by very much.

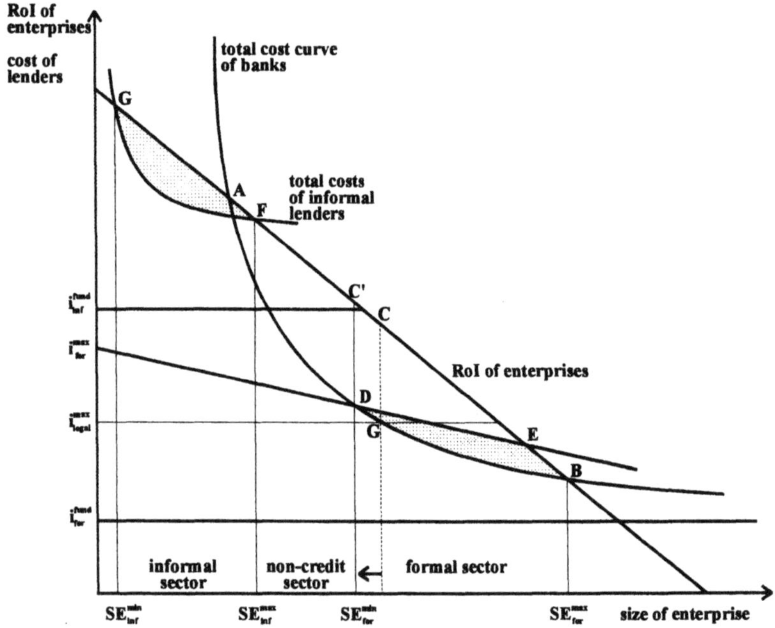

Fig. 17: The credit market following the elimination of interest rate ceilings

Thus, a gap remains in the spectrum of possible enterprise sizes. The constraints to growth have not been eliminated, in particular for small, informal enterprises, which are still unable to expand into the medium-sized enterprise range or become part of the formal sector. One must also ask how useful it would be to expand the formal sector downwards, since, initially at least, no enterprises of this size even exist. It continues to be difficult to start new formal businesses, as new enterprises must still be quite sizeable even when they are founded; in other words, micro and small businesses cannot grow into the medium-sized range "organically". Nonetheless, it is now easier for large enterprises to contract and move down the size range should such an adjustment become necessary on account of unfavourable overall conditions.

Mirroring the findings of this analysis, practical experience in various countries has shown that liberalising the credit market does not automatically lead to a situation in which banks will cater for the financing needs of small enterprises. Indeed, they would usually rather deposit excess liquidity in accounts at the central bank which earn no interest than use it to lend to small enterprises. The segmentation of the credit market which originally arose as a result of the policy of interest rate subsidisation is thus stable, and it constitutes a sufficient condition for the continued existence of all of the effects of credit market segmentation that have been derived in Part II.

Part III. Approaches Taken By Successful Small Loan Programmes

The first two parts of this study analysed the causes and impacts of credit market segmentation. Part III will examine possible ways of reducing segmentation effectively over the long term. However, it cannot be assumed that merely implementing the "solutions" presented here will be sufficient to put an end to dualistic structures, as the continued existence of the informal sector is undoubtedly attributable to a number of other factors as well. In particular, these include bureaucratic obstacles to formalisation as well as excessively strict, overly-complicated regulations and requirements; indeed, complying with these requirements would put many small and micro enterprises out of business. Trimming back the relevant regulations to the extent that micro enterprises would realistically be able to comply with them is thus another necessary condition for the elimination of segmentation. However, a more detailed examination of this topic would go beyond the intended focus of this study.

But, if segmentation is to be eliminated, it is also clear that enterprises cannot continue to be subject to credit rationing on the basis of size. As long as credit rationing –as described in Part I – is still in effect, factor markets will necessarily remain segmented. Thus, eliminating or at least reducing the extent of credit rationing is a necessary condition for sustainable, organic development in any economy. To this end, small loan programmes which are designed to deepen local financial markets and enhance their efficiency have been set up in the framework of international development co-operation activities.

In the following, a theoretical explanation of the impacts of various approaches will be provided. The author has deliberately chosen not to furnish a detailed description of how these approaches work in practice. On the one hand, the specific know-how required for their implementation has already been widely disseminated, as indicated by the large number of successful credit projects that have been carried out using the lending methodologies and institutional strategies outlined below;[45] on the other, as an entire book could be written on each of these options, an in-depth examination of the individual approaches would surely go beyond the scope of the present study.

The first chapter contains a brief overview of the various *strategies* that can be employed to improve the efficiency of credit markets. The subsequent

---

45 Examples of successful small-scale lending projects are the Grameen Bank in Bangladesh, KUPEDES in Indonesia, CERUDEB in Uganda, Calpia in El Salvador and Caja de los Andes in Bolivia.

chapters then show which *instruments* can be used to pursue each of these strategies, and the impacts they have in conjunction with the various strategies. The second chapter explores ways of increasing the propensity to save; this is followed by a discussion of measures geared to enhancing borrowers' ability to pay (Chapter 3) and their willingness to pay (Chapter 4). The final chapter focuses on the institutional options that can be employed to implement the various strategies and instruments in practice.

1. Overview

In Part I of this study, we determined that asymmetric information can prevent even competitive credit markets from clearing, which will in turn induce the banks to subject enterprises within a certain size range to credit rationing. However, whether this will in fact occur depends on the prevailing market conditions, i.e. the presence of certain sets of conditions can lead to other, more favourable outcomes. This chapter briefly outlines various strategies which can be used to influence conditions in credit markets in such a way as to improve the intermediation between borrowers and lenders.

Figure 18 depicts the effects of an increase in both the propensity to save and the ability to pay. A *greater propensity to save*, represented by S(r)', shifts the savings function to the left, which increases the credit supply at every market interest rate. This yields the credit supply function Cr^{S2} (dotted line); consequently, the segment representing the extent to which credit rationing occurs is reduced from CA to EA. Thus, although this will not eliminate the existing information problems, it will reduce the extent of their adverse effects.

Increasing borrowers' *ability to pay* will reduce the risk-related costs incurred by banks that lend to them {represented by the vertical distance between r=i and r(i) and between r=i and r(i)'}. At the same time, the interest rate at which banks can maximise their returns, i^{max}, rises, yielding the credit supply function Cr^{S3} (broken line). The extent of credit rationing is reduced, because the possibility of charging higher interest rates serves to expand the credit supply while simultaneously reducing the demand for credit.

The impacts of *reductions in the banks' transaction costs* are not depicted in the diagram. Transaction costs have the effect of shifting r(i) upward, leading to a corresponding downward shift in Cr^S. A reduction in transaction costs thus causes the credit supply function to shift upwards independent of the interest rate level.

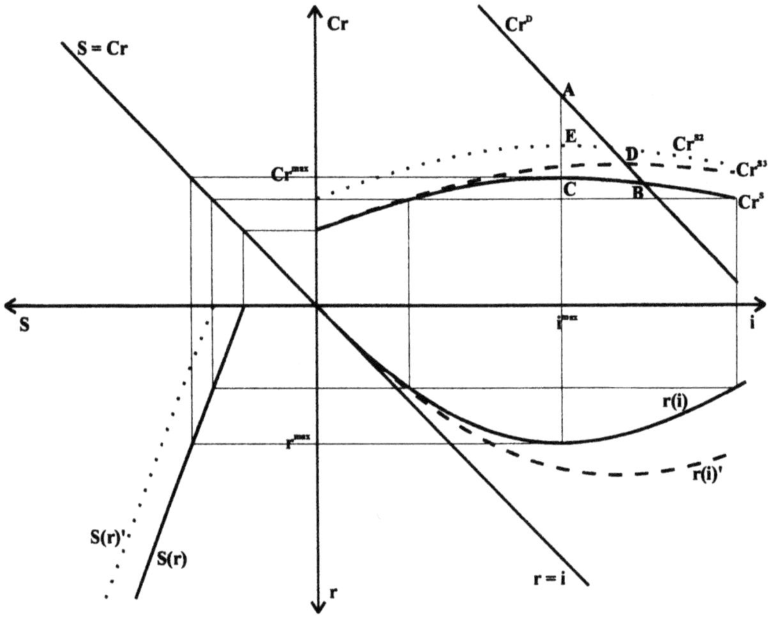

Fig. 18: Reducing credit market segmentation: an overview of the various approaches

Finally, *lowering the costs of enforcing legal claims* can reduce the extent of credit rationing by reducing the minimum size of enterprises to which banks can profitably lend. However, the extent to which credit rationing will be reduced in practice will depend on whether the costs of enforcing legal claims in fact constitute a binding constraint.

2. Increasing the domestic savings volume

As far back as the 1950s, the low propensity to save (within the banking system) in many "developing countries" had already been recognised as a problem.[46] At that time, strategies were implemented to boost the level of savings within national economies through the imposition of tariffs on imports or through inflation. Eventually it became clear that such approaches do not work, and alternative strategies were developed which called for a rise in deposit interest rates with the goal of increasing the savings volume, and thus the credit

46 Cf. McKINNON, 1973.

supply. In the following section, we will consider whether measures of this type can in fact promote this goal. In section (b), other ways of boosting the domestic savings volume will be examined, and in section (c) we will assess the empirical relevance of the problem of an inadequate savings supply.

a) Higher interest rates and the "iron law of savings rate restrictions"

During the era of financial repression, statutory regulations had been passed in many countries which had the effect of making real interest rates negative; this was rightly seen as a situation that needed to be corrected. In the meantime, the consensus view is that deposit interest rates should always be at least high enough to preserve the real value of savers' funds.

However, even after financial systems were liberalised, real interest rates on savings deposits remained slightly negative. This is often attributed to the oligopolistic structures which characterise the banking systems in many countries, and many writers continue to call for rises in deposit rates to ensure that they are at least slightly positive in real terms. Unfortunately, those who advocate such increases often overlook the fact that deposit-taking generates very high transaction costs for the banks, in particular with respect to small-scale deposits. This is due not only to the fact that amounts involved – the average account balances - are very small, but also to the fact that small savers tend to carry out a disproportionate number of transactions on their accounts. At the *Cajas Municipales de Ahorro y Crédito* in Peru, for example it was observed that some micro entrepreneurs deposited all of their cash in their savings accounts at the beginning of their lunch break, and then withdrew it again after they had eaten. As a result, these customers ended up executing as many 10 transactions per day! Although the *Cajas* were able to fund a considerable portion of their loan portfolios with these small deposits, maintenance of small savers' accounts generated annual transaction costs equivalent to more than 30% of the deposit volume mobilised via such accounts.

Given such a cost structure, it is easy to understand why commercial banks will have little interest in deposits of this kind if the interest rate they pay on them is not lower than the cost of acquiring funds from alternative sources by a margin sufficient to offset the transaction costs they incur in mobilising small deposits.

In the following, we will demonstrate how "rational banks" must respond when they are obliged – either by legal regulations or by the pressure of public opinion – to pay a real interest rate of at least 0% on all savings accounts. For this purpose, a model will be used which, for the sake of simplicity, assumes the existence of only two groups of savers: *large-scale savers* save large amounts, and the supply of savings they provide is relatively interest-elastic because it is comparatively easy for them to put their assets in other types of investments, or to invest them abroad. By contrast, *small-scale savers* save small sums, and the supply of savings they provide is relatively interest-inelastic because they hold savings deposits mainly for the purpose of liquidity management or as a kind of emergency reserve to provide against unforeseen future risks, and not as a means of accumulating wealth. In Figure 19, the respective savings supply functions for both small- and large-scale savers are represented by the curves S'_{large} and S'_{small}.

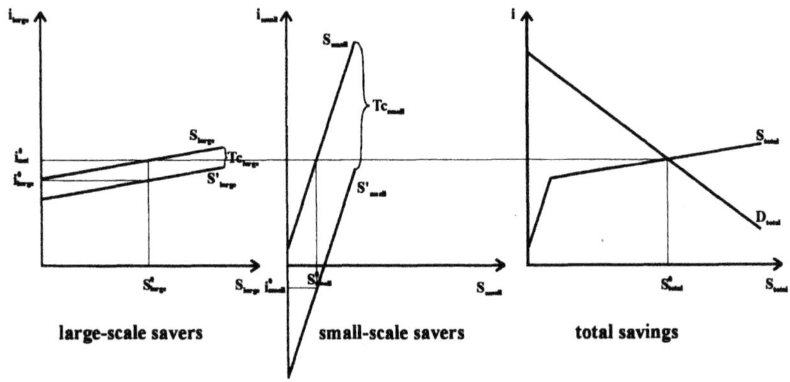

Fig. 19: The savings deposit market in the absence of interest rate restrictions

However, the banks are concerned less with the deposit rate they pay than with the total costs associated with the mobilisation of savings deposits. For this reason, when calculating the costs of raising funds through savings mobilisation they will add their transaction costs to those given by the relevant savings supply functions which have emerged in the market. Addition of these transaction costs causes a parallel upward shift in the supply functions, yielding the total cost curves which are relevant for the banks, namely S_{large} and S_{small}. On the basis of these calculations, the banks will structure their deposit portfolios such that the overall unit costs they incur when mobilising deposits of small-scale savers will be equivalent to those generated by the mobilisation of large-scale deposits.

Assuming that this in the case, S_{total} represents the total savings supply in the financial sector. Given a credit demand function of D_{total} (which has also been adjusted to reflect the relevant transaction costs), the funding costs for the banks would be i^0_{net}. The large-scale savers would deposit S^0_{large} and earn interest of i^0_{large}, while the deposits of small-scale savers would be equal to S^0_{small} and earn a negative real interest rate of i^0_{small}. The market would be in equilibrium, and there would be no "discrimination" against either group of savers.

However, if the banks are obliged by legal regulations or public opinion to pay real interest rates of at least 0% on savings deposits, this will have an impact on their calculations. As is illustrated in Figure 20, statutory lower limits on interest rates have no influence on the market for large-scale savings; as before, the real interest rate paid on these deposits is positive. However, the situation is quite different as regards the market for small-scale deposits: the portion of the market where customers previously saved even when real interest rates were negative is characterised by a supply function which is completely interest-elastic at the minimum interest rate of 0%. In this case, the banks will have to take into account the new total cost function, S_{small}, when performing their calculations.

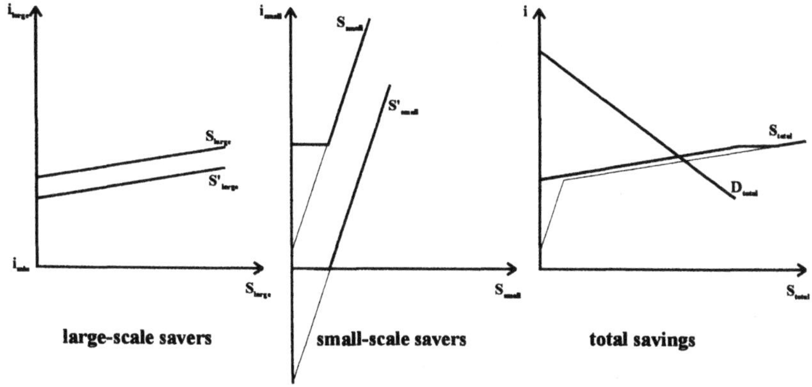

Fig. 20: The savings supply functions given real interest rates of at least 0%

Within the market as a whole, the total cost functions of both segments once again aggregate to form the total supply function S_{total}. Given the presence of the interest-elastic segment in the market for small-scale savings, the total supply function also contains a completely interest-elastic area. However, it is located to the right of the point at which the supply function intersects the demand curve.

The implications of the new situation for the market are shown in Figure 21. In the market as a whole, supply and demand intersect at an interest rate of i^1_{net}. Because the banks will not accept deposits which would generate total costs of more than i^1_{net}, they no longer serve small savers. By contrast, a larger volume of large-scale deposits (S^1_{large}) will be accepted at the interest rate of i^1_{large}, which is higher than that which was previously on offer. As a result, the rents earned by large-scale savers increase by the area shaded in grey. Small-scale savers and those who exhibit a demand for credit are penalised with rent losses, which are also represented by an area shaded in grey.

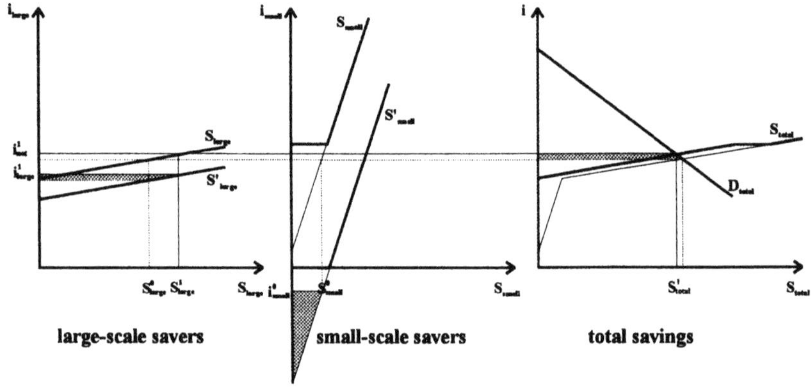

Fig. 21: The effects on the market when real deposit rates are 0% or higher

This analysis shows that attempting to promote small-scale savers by systematically setting deposit rates to preserve the value of all savers' funds is counterproductive, and in fact is detrimental to the very groups in society whom the mandatory minimum interest rates would be intended to help in the first place. For this reason, it is inappropriate to demand the imposition of such minimum rates. Indeed, once one has decided in favour of an economic system based on the market, one must also accept the logical consequences of that decision. And one of these consequences is that the various economic actors will have to bear the specific costs incurred in providing them with the services they demand and obtain via the market. In lending, this view has long since been recognised for what it is – simple common sense. As the same fundamental economic laws that govern the credit market also apply in the savings market, well-intentioned interventions which limit the decision-making autonomy of financial institutions will therefore be counterproductive.

This is not to say that it is acceptable for economic policymakers to take a passive stance. Wherever oligopolistic structures have resulted in X-inefficiencies and unnecessarily high spreads, steps should be taken to eliminate these problems. However, negative real interest rates in themselves do not necessarily indicate the presence of these specific market imperfections. On the contrary: when savers are offered differing interest rates based on the size of their deposits and the term they select, this suggests that deposit products have been designed with customers' interests in mind and tailored to their specific savings needs.

There is a further argument against raising deposit rates as a means of solving the problem of credit rationing, and it has to do with the endogenous nature of the deposit rate. Assuming that the financial sector is not characterised by serious market imperfections and that no excessive monopoly or oligopoly rents are being skimmed off, the deposit rate will emerge "on its own" as a result of market processes. An increase in interest rates which is not induced by the market would not shift the savings supply function itself, but instead lead to "savings rationing". In the Stiglitz-Weiss model – which, after all, already makes allowance for the problem of asymmetric information in the credit market – the deposit rate and the deposit volume also emerge endogenously as a result of market processes. Consequently, intervention in any form will only increase the extent of credit rationing.

b) Other options for increasing the propensity to save

Raising the interest rate is thus not a viable way to increase the propensity to save. In the following we will analyse alternative instruments which make it more attractive – in particular for small-scale savers – to keep their surplus funds in the banking system. To this end, we must first examine in greater detail the various *motives* for saving, following which the results of this examination can be assessed with regard to their implications for the design of more appropriate *terms and conditions* for savings products.

Small-scale savers seldom set aside money for the purpose of *accumulating assets*, as they tend to invest long-term surpluses in their homes, in their children's education, or in their own small enterprises. This is one fundamental difference between the situation in most "developing countries" today and conditions in industrialised countries in the previous century. In Western countries in the 1800s, small-scale savers usually lived in rented apartments of dwellings and were in dependent employment. As a result, they did not need to set aside funds to invest in a home or business, and this in turn enabled financial intermediaries to mobilise considerable sums from a large number of small-scale savers which could then be channelled into the development of large industrial organisations.

When it comes to the long-term application of surplus funds, small-scale savers in most "developing countries" have options which are more attractive to them than what the financial sector can offer. For this reason, they set aside financial reserves primarily for the purpose of *providing against unforeseen future risks*, or as a means of *smoothing out fluctuations in their incomes and expenses*. In either case, the interest rate they will earn plays only a secondary role in their decision to make use of a particular option, although the level of interest it will generate naturally affects their incomes. It is far more important for a small saver to be able to access his savings easily and quickly, perhaps even immediately. For example, a family member might become ill on a Saturday, or an entrepreneur might wish to take advantage of a particularly promising business opportunity which has arisen unexpectedly over the weekend, and which cannot wait until Monday. In such situations, small-scale savers need to be able to access their savings immediately, i.e. outside of the banks' normal opening hours. For this reason, reducing waiting times and extending the financial institutions' opening hours will do far more to boost the volume of deposits collected from small-scale savers than even a quite substantial increase in the interest rate. Therefore, when not only the interest rate offered, but also the liquidity of funds on deposit, differs greatly depending on the size of the deposits involved, this is not so much a sign of discrimination against the poor as it is an indication that range of deposit products provided by a given financial institution have been designed with customers' specific needs and preferences in mind.

c) The empirical relevance of the problem of insufficient savings

The financial systems of most countries were liberalised a number of years ago, either because of the unfavourable consequences of *financial repression* or in response to pressure brought to bear by the Bretton Woods institutions. Since then, lending decisions have been based more on economic criteria than on political considerations, and relatively competitive markets for savings deposits have emerged. As a result, formal financial institutions have become increasingly liquid, and presently have more liquidity than they require to fund their lending activities.[47]

---

[47] For El Salvador, cf. MOMMARTZ/SCHMIDT, 1996, p. 5; for the West African monetary union, cf. CAMARA, 1998, p. 177. In 1994, reserves held by Malian banks at the Central Bank were between 12 and 56 times higher than the minimum reserve requirements.

Nonetheless, experience has shown that many banks either do not grant small loans at all, or issue such loans on such an insignificant scale that it is clear they have no interest in serving this segment of the market.

Previous strategies for alleviating credit rationing by increasing the propensity to save were based on the STIGLITZ/WEISS model. In order to explain the obvious inconsistency between this model and the empirical findings, we will now return to the expanded Stiglitz-Weiss model as presented in Part I. As in Figure 7, an explicit distinction is drawn between large- and small-scale borrowers. Figure 22 provides an explanation for the "refusal" of the banks to lend to the microenterprise sector on any appreciable scale.

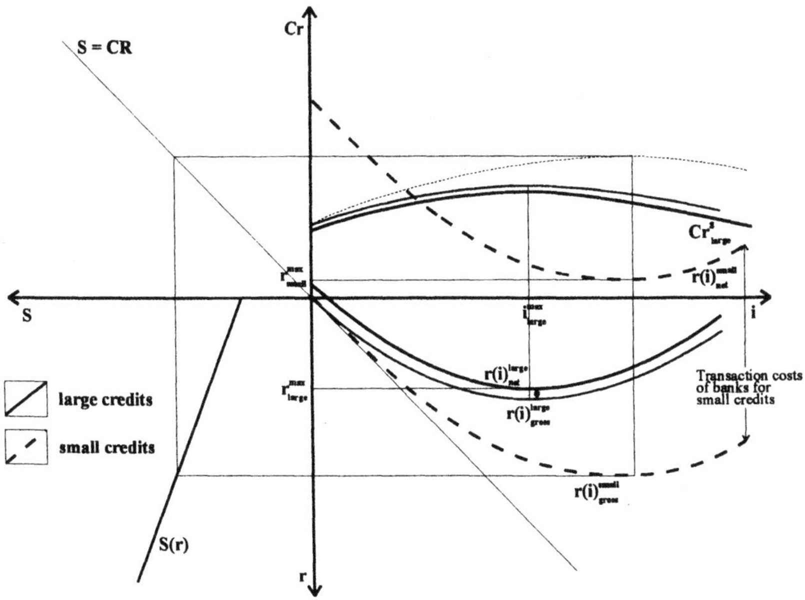

Fig. 22: The small loan supply provided by a liquid banking sector

Even if a financial institution is so liquid that the opportunity costs of using available funds to make additional loans work out to 0, it will only issue additional loans if it can avoid incurring losses in the process. Figure 22 shows a set of market conditions in which small loans generate such high transaction and risk-related costs that even in the best case, the banks would earn a negative net return. Given these conditions, lending to the micro enterprise sector can only have adverse consequences for the banks. For this reason, they will refrain from granting small loans even if they have ample liquidity. Thus, increasing the propensity to save will not solve the problem of credit rationing.

3. Measures for enhancing the ability to pay

It is of paramount importance to any lender that borrowers be both able and willing to pay back their loans. These two parameters are interrelated, i.e. an improvement in the ability to pay will generally have a positive effect on the willingness to pay, while a very high willingness to pay will influence borrowers' financial decisions such that when the time comes to meet obligations to lenders, they will more likely be in a position to pay. While the willingness and the ability to pay will be examined separately in the following because such a division is useful for analytical purposes, this should not obscure the fact that all of the measures presented below influence both parameters. However, the analysis can, and will, be limited to an examination of the principal direct effects on the ability to pay.

The first section describes the effects of a reduction in information asymmetries. Although such a reduction will not alter the ability to pay of any individual enterprise, it will enable credit institutions to screen potential borrowers more effectively by making it easier to recognise applicants who are not creditworthy. The second section discusses the effects of intertemporal incentives, which mitigate the negative effects of asymmetric information, although they do not alter the extent of the informational asymmetries themselves. The third section examines the ways in which the transaction costs incurred by the banks influence their customers' ability to pay. Chapter 3 concludes with an analysis of the importance of the economic environment.

a) Reducing information asymmetries

Asymmetric information is *the prime* cause of market-induced credit rationing. In addition to increasing the probability that borrowers will default on their loans, it gives rise to adverse selection and moral hazard; these in turn lead to the emergence of an implicit interest rate ceiling, above which a bank cannot lend without causing its own return to drop. This limits the scope of the bank's lending activities, and many of those who demand credit will be subject to rationing.

Thus, if the problem of credit rationing is to be overcome, one must begin by attempting to reduce information asymmetries. The method of credit analysis traditionally used by banks is not well-suited to reducing such asymmetries when dealing with small and micro enterprises. For one thing, it presupposes the existence of formal structures such those needed to develop reliable accounting practices, and in addition it distinguishes between business and family expenses, which is not appropriate with respect to this sector. Because the analysis is performed mainly at the bank on the basis of written documents, the loan officer cannot form his own opinion of the situation, which gives loan applicants substantial leeway to "stretch the truth" when providing information, thereby aggravating the problem of asymmetric information considerably. For this reason, some banks require their customers to have an independent auditor provide written certification of the accuracy of all financial and business data; however, this pushes the transaction costs for small loans to absurdly high levels, given the amounts involved. In short, the banks' traditional approach to credit analysis will inevitably fail to resolve the problem of asymmetric information when used in the micro enterprise sector, and thus its use will effectively prevent the banks from seeing lending to this sector as a potentially profitable line of business.

However, other credit analysis concepts which are more appropriate to the situation of microentrepreneurs have already been developed and tested in real lending situations; they have also been continuously improved and refined on the basis of practical experience. This experience has shown that the inability to pay is seldom attributable to external shocks, but is nearly always the result of faulty credit analysis (in conjunction with the fact that borrowers tend to overestimate their own debt capacity). Therefore, appropriate credit analysis is *the prime* instrument for ensuring that borrowers will be able to repay their loans.

Credit analysis which is adapted to the requirements of micro enterprises begins by taking stock of the financial situation of a potential borrower's *family economic unit*, consisting of both the enterprise and the household. To this end, the loan officer goes to the entrepreneur's place of business and/or home and gathers all relevant data, i.e. all data on income and expenditures, both within the business and within the household. The information obtained must cover both areas because when deciding how to spend any surpluses generated by the business, the entrepreneur will naturally give priority to expenditures related to the family's basic needs. The borrower's ability to pay is then calculated on the basis of the residual surplus, i.e. what is left over after such essential family expenses have been met, and this ensures that he will be able to pay even if the project to be financed by the loan does not lead to an increase in income. As a result, it is unnecessary to monitor the borrower's activities to verify that the disbursed funds are being used for the intended purpose, which, as experience has shown, is scarcely feasible in any case.[48]

After performing a detailed analysis, experienced loan officers can often assess the financial situation of micro entrepreneurs more accurately than the entrepreneurs themselves. This is attributable first of all to the structured and relatively comprehensive collection of data on all payment flows, and secondly to the fact that performing the analysis at the applicants' place of business and/or residence makes it quite difficult for them to provide incorrect information. Micro entrepreneurs often do not have a precise overview of their own financial situation, and experienced loan officers can enhance the amount and quality of information available to both borrower and lender by asking very specific questions. Thus, a good credit analysis technique not only reduces the extent of *asymmetrical information*, but also increases the overall *level of information*, thus effectively ensuring that borrowers will not become overindebted.

An empirical discussion of the effects of reduced information asymmetries will not be presented here, as successful credit institutions use a combination of various instruments to ensure that loans are paid back on time, and the favourable results cannot be directly ascribed to the individual instruments. Instead, the effects will be discussed from a theoretical perspective using the models introduced in Part I.

Figure 23 shows how a reduction in information asymmetries will effect the banks' lending activities. The improved amount and quality of information available to them makes it easier for banks to recognise when customers are not creditworthy, and thus to exclude them from access to credit. This in turn reduces their risk-related costs, which in the diagram correspond to the vertical distance between r=i and r(i) and between r=i and r(i'). Because the problem of adverse selection has now been mitigated, the interest rate at which banks can maximise their return increases from i^{max} to $i^{max\ 2}$. This extends the entire credit supply function upwards and to the right (Cr^{S2}). The total volume of loans disbursed increases from Cr^{max} to $Cr^{max\ 2}$; in addition, the higher interest rates charged in the market will cause the demand for credit to drop. The end result is that excess demand for credit and the extent of credit rationing will decrease from CA to ED.

48 Cf. LIPTON, 1976, p. 547.

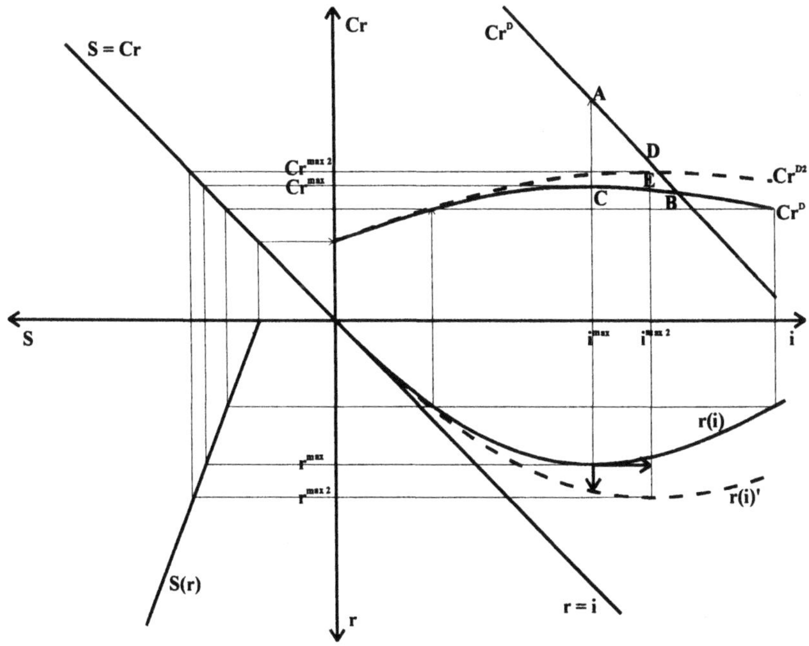

Fig. 23: Effects of reduced information asymmetry as depicted by the Stiglitz/Weiss model

If one looks at how the market functions for enterprises of different sizes (as is the case with the basic model), one can see that the improved information situation enables the banks to charge higher interest rates on loans to enterprises of every size without undermining their own returns. This causes the interest rate ceiling function to rotate away from the X-axis; in addition, the banks' total costs will decrease because they no longer have to assume the same level of risk, in particular for loans to small enterprises. The contract area increases by the area shaded in grey from DBE' to GBE, i.e. it is now economically feasible for the banks to serve enterprises which fall into the size range defined by $SE_{for}^{min 2}$ and SE_{for}^{min}. Consequently, these enterprises now have access to bank loans, and the lower range of the spectrum of enterprise sizes which are eligible for loans has been extended downward.

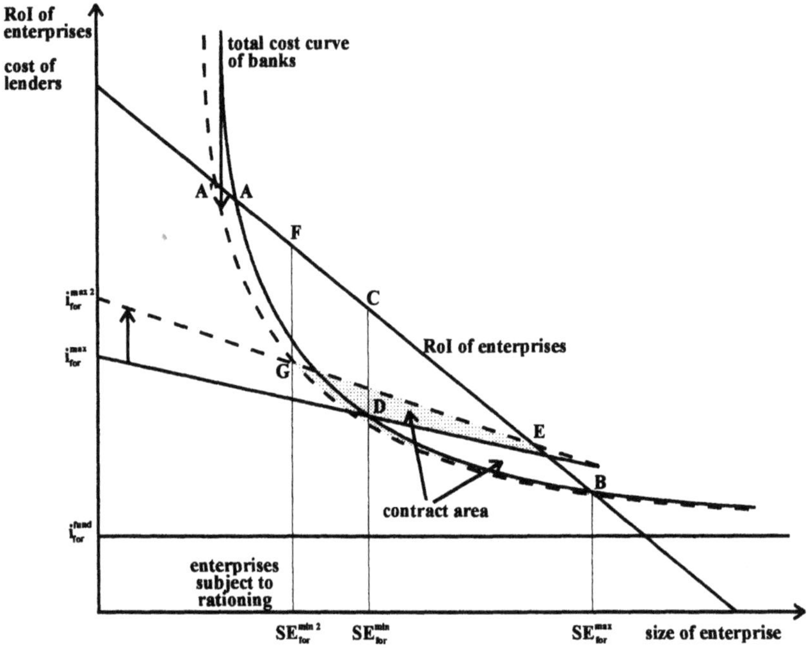

Fig. 24: Effects of reduced information asymmetry as depicted by the basic model

b) Mitigating the information problem through intertemporal incentives

"In markets with important moral hazard problems, competitive behaviour, in general, features intertemporal linkages."[49] *Intertemporal linkages* are said to exist when the utility of a business relationship applies not only to the present, but to the future as well, and when the continuation of that relationship is contingent on the good behaviour of the parties involved.

Enterprises are more competitive if they can borrow in the formal sector, and it is of great importance to them to have assured access to credit over the long term. Indeed, the utility of future access to credit often exceeds the amount of current outstanding loans. A bank can turn this situation to its own advantage by promising its customers that they will be able to take out loans in the future, but only on condition that they pay back their current outstanding loans on time.

49 STIGLITZ/WEISS, 1983, p. 925.

However, intertemporal linkages are only effective if a number of basic conditions have been fulfilled. For one thing, they will only function if overall economic conditions are fairly stable and the environment in which micro entrepreneurs operate is not overly hostile – i.e., such linkages will only function if micro entrepreneurs have prospects of earning profits over the long term. Otherwise, future credits will not be as valuable to them.

Secondly, borrowers must be convinced that it is in fact feasible to maintain a long-term credit relationship with a financial institution. For example, if the interest charged on loans is not sufficient to cover the costs incurred in providing them, borrowers will quickly begin to suspect that at some point in the future the bank will either have to begin rationing credit, or else cease its operations entirely. Uncertainty of any type with respect to the provision of future loans gives borrowers a strong incentive to refuse to pay back their current loans. The history of small loan programmes is replete with examples of this phenomenon.

A third important factor is how serious the bank is about collecting loans which are in arrears. The resolute enforcement of legal claims signals, on the one hand, that the credit relationship is seen as a business relationship and not as a form of assistance intended to advance social-welfare goals. This in turn increases borrowers' confidence that the institution will continue to exist over the long term. At the same time, the "value" of refusing to pay will diminish because borrowers can see that at some point they will have no choice but to pay.

Finally, it is important for credit institutions to recognise very quickly when loans have fallen into arrears, and to act without delay to collect overdue instalments. Such behaviour indicates that the institution is a serious, professionally run operation, and in addition increases the probability that borrowers will be able to repay their loans. Micro entrepreneurs in particular seldom miss a payment because they genuinely do not have the required funds, but rather because, in their eyes, other expenses take precedence at that particular moment. Experience has shown that repayment rates can be increased considerably if, after a borrower has missed a payment, the loan officer visits him at his place of business the very next day and uses all appropriate means to induce him to pay. The borrower is then often able to make the payment by diverting the funds from other applications. Because the arrears problem was not serious enough to jeopardise access to future loans, the intertemporal incentives remain in effect.

Intertemporal linkages do not reduce information asymmetries. However, they do mitigate the problems created by such asymmetries because they bring the interests of credit customers into line with those of the credit institutions. Thus, in taking decisions with respect to their finances, borrowers will act out of "self-interest" and ensure that are able to repay their loans because future loans are very valuable to them, and they wish to avoid jeopardising their continued access to this source of credit. This eliminates or at least considerably reduces the problem of moral hazard. Of course, there will also be a corresponding increase in the willingness to pay.

Alleviating information problems enables the banks to lower their risk-related costs while raising their interest rates, thereby reducing the minimum size of enterprises to which they can profitably lend. A theoretical explanation of how intertemporal incentives work will not be provided here, as the effects of such incentives are similar to those of reduced information asymmetries and thus can be inferred from Figures 23 and 24 in the preceding section.

c) Reducing the transaction costs of banks

The transaction costs generated by loans to the micro enterprise sector are so high that they often prevent this market segment from being served in the first place. The credit technology used by traditional banks would result in costs of over 100% (per annum) of the amount of small, short-term loans, which is why the banks do not even attempt to develop credit facilities that would enable them to offer loans to micro enterprises on a cost-covering basis. In any case, the conditions of such loans would be even less attractive than those in the informal credit sector.

However, banks can reduce their transaction costs by employing suitable credit technologies and streamlining their organisational structures. Special custom-tailored software enables banks to develop a high-volume, "mass-market" lending business in the micro enterprise sector, and thus to achieve economies of scale, which in turn can reduce transaction costs to less than 20% of the loan amount.[50] Compared to the costs associated with conventional – i.e. larger – bank loans, this is still a very high figure; however, it is no longer so high as to preclude successful small-scale lending. Cost coverage is achieved at real interest rates of around 30%, which is considerably less than the real interest rates charged in the informal credit sector, making such loans extremely attractive for micro entrepreneurs.

Figure 25 shows how reduced transaction costs influence the banks' lending decisions. In order to separate transaction costs from risk-related costs, a cost

50 See, for example, Caja de los Andes in Bolivia or Calpiá in El Salvador.

function which does not take risk-related costs into account (TCC without risk-related costs) has been plotted alongside the total cost curve of the banks. A reduction in transaction costs shifts this function toward the origin (TCC' without risk-related costs). To arrive at the new total costs figure, the risk-related costs must be incorporated into this function. However, a reduction in transaction costs leads to lower interest rates, which in turn mitigate information problems and thus reduce risk-related costs. Consequently, the vertical distance between the total cost curve and the function which does not account for risk-related is reduced for enterprises of every size.

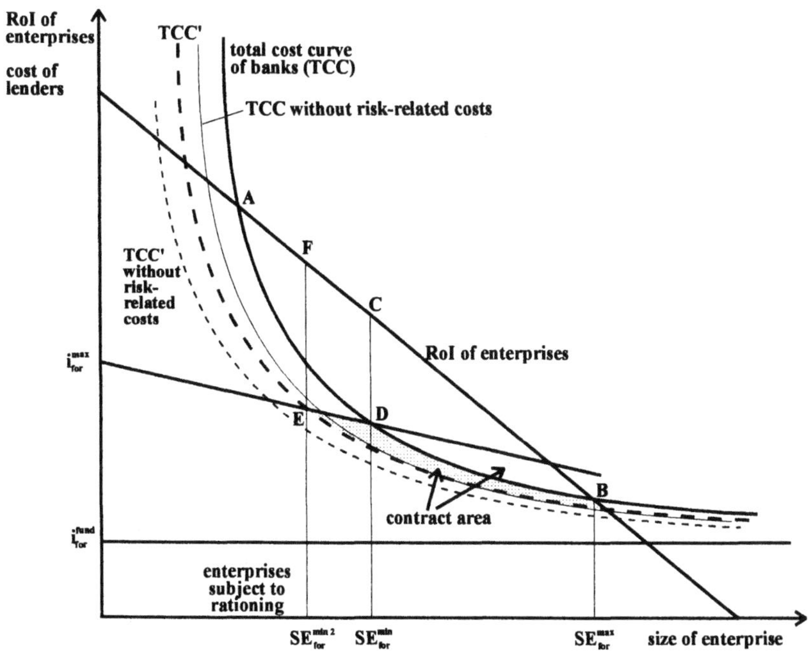

Fig. 25: The effect of reduced transaction costs in the basic model

In relative terms, the banks' total costs thus drop by more than its transaction costs, which results in a lopsided expansion of lending which benefits smaller enterprises more than larger ones, thus causing the segment of the total enterprise size range which is subject to credit rationing to contract. In the example shown here, the contract area increases by the area shaded in grey (EBD). Owing to the reduction in transaction costs, enterprises whose size ranges from $SE_{for}^{min\,2}$ to SE_{for}^{min} now have access to credit.

d) An improvement in the overall economic environment

All economic activity takes place within a broad social and economic context which plays a role in determining whether a given activity will be successful. Although individual financial institutions cannot influence the overall economic environment, it nonetheless has a considerable impact on the earnings prospects of enterprises, and thus on their ability to pay. Thus, in this section we will examine the effects of an improved economic environment on supply and demand in the credit market; however, ways of improving the economic environment will not be analysed. For the sake of simplicity, we shall define an improved economic environment as one in which the economy as a whole is more stable and the earnings prospects of enterprises are improved.

The first effect of a more stable overall economy is that the distribution pattern of profit ratios in the enterprise sector will become less dispersed. This tends to reduce information asymmetries because asymmetric information distribution is a particularly serious problem when profit ratios exhibit a high degree of dispersion.[51] In addition, in a more stable overall environment an enterprise is more likely to earn profits which are roughly in line with those it earned in previous periods; this further reduces information asymmetries, at least for subsequent loans. Enterprises can thus plan with greater certainty and more easily estimate the profits that will be generated by projects financed with future loans, which means that, in their eyes, the value of loans which would be available later on will increase. Consequently, the banks will be able to employ intertemporal incentives more effectively to enhance the willingness to pay. Additionally, the improvement in the earnings prospects of enterprises will also have a direct positive impact on borrowers' ability to pay.

In Figure 26, the effects of an improved economic environment have been incorporated into the STIGLITZ/WEISS model. First of all, as a result of the effects described above, the return function of the banks r(i) flattens out somewhat so that it extends further downwards. The reduction in risk-related costs, combined with potentially higher interest rates, in turn cause(s) the credit supply function Cr^S to rise more steeply to the right. This means that, so far, the effects are analogous to those of reduced information asymmetries.

However, an improved economic environment will also shift the credit demand function (Cr^D) to the right, as investments will now yield a higher return. An expansion in the credit supply thus causes the demand for credit to increase. As a result, it is unclear what the overall effect on the extent of credit

---

[51] Cf. STIGLITZ/WEISS, 1981.

rationing will be: in the example shown below, the extent of credit rationing is reduced somewhat, from CA to ED.

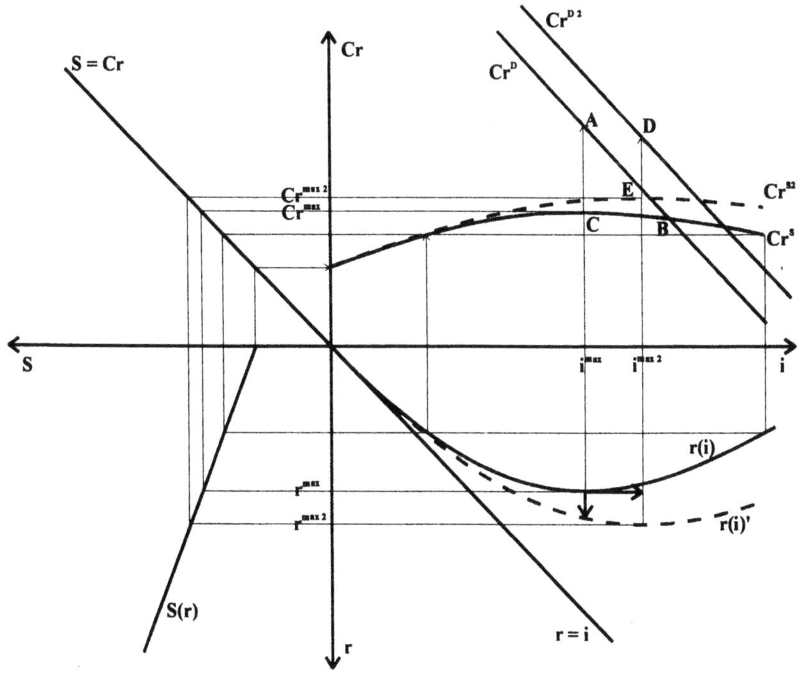

Fig. 26: The effect of an improved economic environment as depicted in the STIGLITZ/ WEISS model

Analysing the situation using the basic model enables us to assess more accurately the effects of an improved economic environment. We will begin with the *direct* effects, which are depicted in Figure 27 and are similar to the effects of a reduction in information asymmetries: the interest rate ceiling line rotates upward, while the total cost function of the banks rotates downward. In addition, the RoI function of the enterprises shifts upward. Therefore, the direct result would be that the contract area would expand to include the area shaded in grey, i.e. it would increase from DBE to GB'E'.

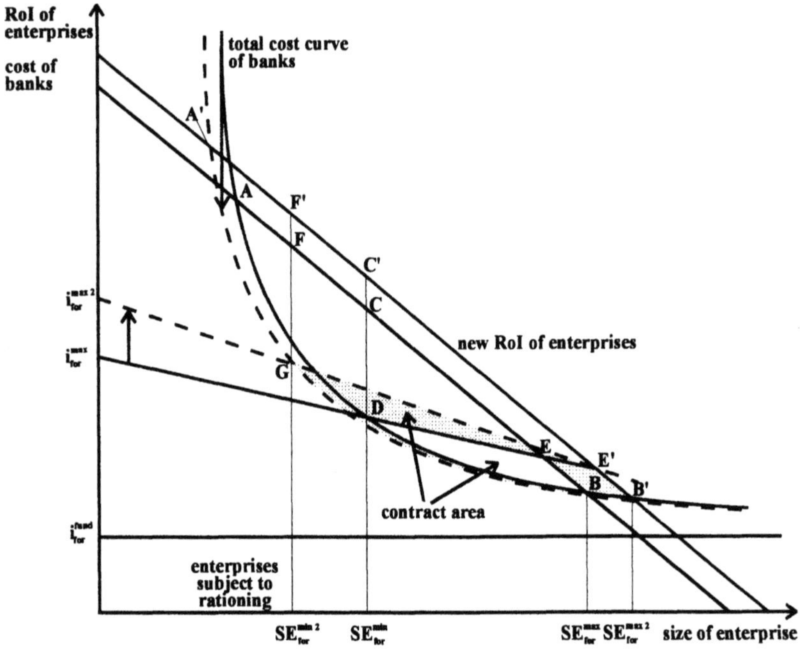

Fig. 27: The direct effects of an improved economic environment as depicted by the basic model

However, it is unlikely that such an expansion in lending activities would have no influence on funding costs in the formal financial sector. For this reason, in Figure 28, the *indirect* effect of a (moderate) increase in the cost of funds from i_{for}^{fund} to i_{for}^{fund2} has been incorporated into the analysis. The result is an upward parallel shift in the total cost function of the banks, irrespective of enterprise size. This function is depicted in Figure 27 as a broken line, and its new position is designated in Figure 28 as the solid line TCC'(i_{for}^{fund2}). The contract area is altered, changing from DBE to GB'. It is unclear what effect this will have on enterprises at the upper end of the size spectrum, as a substantial increase in funding costs can also cause the maximum size to decrease. By contrast, it is clear that the lower end of the size range will be extended downward to include even smaller enterprises, as funding costs account for a considerably smaller share of total lending costs in this size range. On the other hand, though, reducing the extent of information problems lowers risk-related costs and increases the maximum interest rate to an extent that is more than sufficient to offset the rise in funding costs.

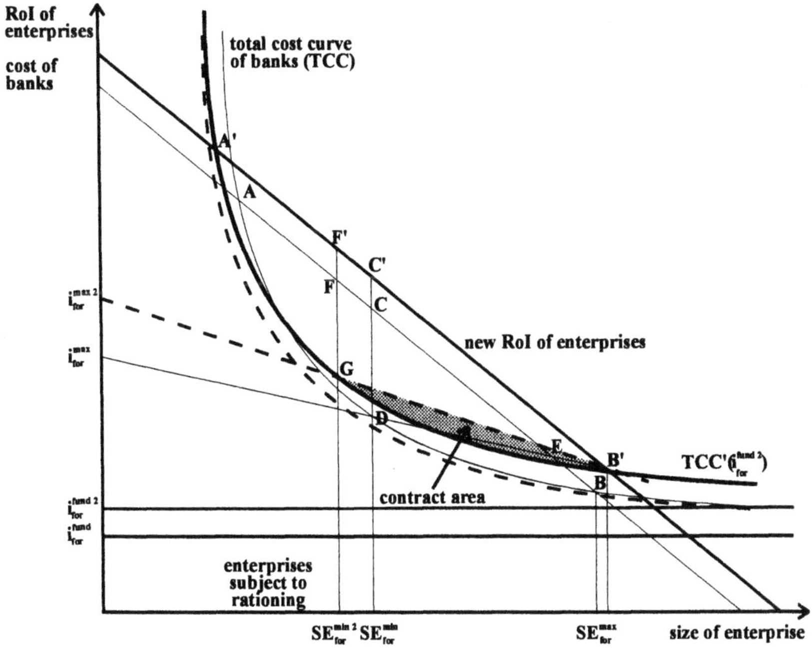

Fig. 28: The overall effects of an improved economic environment

The overall effect of an improved economic environment on credit rationing is clearly favourable. Large enterprises are not subject to rationing, and thus any decline in lending to businesses at the upper end of the size range will be due simply to the fact that enterprises decide against taking out loans because of the high level of interest rates. Moreover, the extent of rationing with respect to medium-sized enterprises is reduced. Thus, the overall effect of an improved economic environment on credit rationing is unambiguously positive.

4. Measures for enhancing the willingness to pay

The ability to pay does not in itself ensure that a loan will be repaid – the borrower must also be willing to pay. Therefore, this chapter examines measures which can increase a borrower's willingness to pay. The first section describes various aspects which determine a borrower's intrinsic motivation in the narrower sense (cf. Part I); section 2 examines the scope for increasing intrinsic motivation in the broader sense by bringing peer pressure to bear. The third section presents various approaches for reducing the costs which the banks incur when enforcing claims, and thus for increasing the extrinsic motivation to repay loans. Although intertemporal incentives also enhance extrinsic motivation, they will not be discussed here, as their effects on the ability to pay were described in the preceding chapter. The final section analyses the ways in which a reduction in the costs of enforcing legal claims will impact bank lending.

a) Mentality, attitudes, cultural aspects and social proximity

In some countries or regions, the *mentality* of borrowers is such that, for ethical reasons, they would not think of refusing to pay back a loan. If a financial institution can make use of such a mentality in credit relationships, this will clearly be the easiest and least expensive way of ensuring that its clients will be willing to pay. However, the way of thinking which characterises a given mentality is something which has evolved over centuries and can only be changed with difficulty and over a long period of time. Consequently, it must be regarded primarily as a characteristic of the local "operating environment", and thus as a given and not as an instrument which can be used to enhance the willingness to pay.

The prevailing *attitudes* toward credit relationships are also a product of historical experience. In many rural regions, credit relationships have traditionally been part of "patronage systems", i.e., broader landowner-tenant relationships often based on a form of sharecropping and perhaps also involving features of the manorial system. In such areas, it is taken for granted that borrowers will only pay their creditors "what they can spare", i.e. their available surpluses. Paying debts back in the form of regular instalments of a fixed amount would seem absurd to them. Instead, they might offer to pay back part of their debts "in kind" by providing their labour or political support; however, such payments "in kind" tend to be of little value to banks. Moreover, the lender is clearly expected to provide new loans, e.g. to finance weddings and permit participation in important social events, even if the borrower's outstanding loans are already substantially overdue. In such a setting, it is nearly impossible for formal financial institutions to develop a successful small-scale lending business.

In many regions, repayment discipline has been undermined by credit programmes implemented in the past which did not rigorously enforce their claims on borrowers. For example, a state-owned development bank in Bangladesh achieved a repayment rate of barely 10% in urban areas of that country.[52] As a result, borrowers came to regard loans as transfer payments

52 Cf. JACKELEN/RHYNE, , 1991, p.5.

which were intended to "help the poor" as part of government social-welfare activities, rather than as legally binding debts that actually had to be repaid. Such an attitude naturally makes it more difficult for a financial institution to succeed that wishes to grant small loans on a commercially viable, sustainable basis.

However, borrowers' attitudes toward credit are somewhat easier to influence than their mentality. Prior to the disbursement of funds, the bank needs to explain to loan applicants in no uncertain terms that if they refuse to pay, it will attempt to compel them to pay using all appropriate means at their disposal. If the bank later "practices what it preaches" in a clear, understandable and resolute manner, borrowers' attitudes will quickly change. However, implementation of such a strategy will generate additional costs for the bank during the initial phase of lending operations.

Cultural aspects can pose a decisive obstacle to lending. However, because they differ from country to country and are very difficult to change, we will look at just one example which illustrates the absolute necessity of analysing the relevant cultural setting before attempting to implement a project. In Mali, even well-educated people who have attended French universities believe that sorcerers have the power to make people ill if they so desire. Consequently, borrowers often prevent banks from enforcing the repayment of loans by intimidating the responsible credit staff, which they do by threatening to have "their" sorcerers make the staff members ill. Because they are afraid of the sorcerers, this tactic effectively prevents bank employees from taking steps to collect overdue loans, and thus there is no chance that financial institutions will be able build up a successful, i.e. commercially viable lending business.

In Part I, we demonstrated that the lender's *social proximity* to the borrower (or the lack thereof) exerts an important influence on the latter's repayment behaviour. The repayment of loans is given a much higher priority if the social distance between the borrower and the lending institution is small. Thus, in small-scale lending operations, proper "social positioning" is one of the most effective means of increasing borrowers' intrinsic motivation to repay loans.

Social proximity can be increased in a number of ways. For one thing, not only loan officers, but other staff members as well – including management – should be recruited from the local population. It is important for customers to feel that they know the financial institution well, and that it knows them well; the institution will have achieved this if loan officers establish personal relationships with borrowers, if the financial products are geared to the needs of the customers, and if the loan officers visit the borrowers at their business premises or in their homes on a regular basis. Finally, it is useful to appoint micro entrepreneurs who are well-known among the members of the target group to the supervisory board, as this is the body that sets the long-term policies of the financial institution. Having such representatives of the target group serve on the supervisory board not only increases the extent to which the other micro entrepreneurs will identify with "their" bank; it also ensures that the institution will remain committed to serving the micro enterprise sector over the long term.

b) Peer pressure

In many rural regions of Asia, the use of peer pressure has proven to be an effective instrument for ensuring the willingness to pay; the best-known example is the Grameen Bank.[53] By contrast, attempts use peer pressure in the same way in urban areas of Latin America have failed in almost every case. In this section, the mechanisms involved in peer pressure will be described so that we can then define the necessary conditions for the successful use of this instrument, and also explain why it was bound to fail in the urban context of Latin America.[54]

If peer pressure is to be brought to bear, a credit group must first be formed. While a number of institutions oblige the individual group members to assume liability for the repayment of loans disbursed to other group members, or make further access to credit contingent on punctual repayment on the part of all group members, the Grameen Bank merely asks group members "to influence the ... repayment behaviour"[55] of borrowers who are unwilling to repay their loans. The ostracism which delinquent borrowers will have to face if they refuse to pay increases their intrinsic motivation (in the broader sense) to meet their obligations after all. In the case of the Grameen Bank, this tactic is effective even though the other persons in the group do not suffer any adverse economic consequences whatsoever if one member refuses to pay, i.e. access to future loans does not depend on the behaviour of the other group members.[56] However, the social proximity of the Grameen Bank to its target group is so great that if one member refuses to pay, the others in the group see this as weakening "their" institution, and thus ostracise borrowers who are unwilling to pay. Because the latter are unwilling to risk being regarded as "social outcasts" within their respective village communities, they will enter into the credit relationship with

---

[53] For example, cf. PEEGE, 1988, p. 167.

[54] Cf. SCHMIDT/ZEITINGER 1994, pp. 64-70.

[55] SCHMIDT/ZEITINGER, 1994, p. 62.

[56] Cf. SCHMIDT/ZEITINGER, 1994, p. 62.

the intention of meeting their obligations; hence, unwillingness to pay is effectively ruled out as a risk factor.

However, peer pressure is only effective under certain circumstances. First of all, it is necessary for group members to be truly capable of distinguishing between the inability to pay and the unwillingness to pay, which requires a relatively intimate knowledge of the economic and social situation of the other group members. In stable rural areas, residents of a village usually know each other so well that they already possess such information, and do not first have to procure it. By contrast, micro entrepreneurs in the urban regions of Latin America know each other only superficially, and thus it is difficult – if not impossible – for them to judge whether the other group members will be able to meet their obligations.

Secondly, if peer pressure is to be brought to bear, ostracism by the other group members must go hand in hand with tangible unfavourable consequences for borrowers who are unwilling to pay. In stable rural regions, the potential exclusion of the borrower from the village community is a sufficient threat. In the urban areas of Latin America, however, there are few bonds between individual micro entrepreneurs, and the potential threat of ostracism does not serve as a particularly effective deterrent.

Lastly, peer pressure can only work within the context of a relatively stable economic environment in which changing one's occupation and moving to a new location would be prohibitively expensive. In Latin America, micro entrepreneurs often pick up and move on their own initiative, trying out various locations in completely different parts of a given city or even in different cities, in the hope that they will be able to increase their incomes by operating in a new setting. By moving to a new location, borrowers who are unwilling to pay can easily escape from any social monitoring on the part of the persons who make up their immediate "business environment", thus making it difficult to "punish" uncooperative behaviour.

The effectiveness of peer pressure as an instrument for ensuring the willingness to pay is thus particularly dependent on the environment in which a financial institution operates. The borrowers in a group must know each other well, their lives must be lived in a stable network of social relationships, and they must have little opportunity to pick up and move. These conditions are more likely to exist in rural regions than in cities, where the micro enterprise sector must adapt to constantly changing circumstances – which in itself frequently induces them to take up a new occupation or move to a new location.

c) Reducing the costs of foreclosure and liquidation of collateral

If the enforcement of claims gives rise to high costs, this can undermine borrowers' extrinsic motivation to repay loans. If the costs of recovering overdue loans exceed the loan amount and a financial institution is unable to pass these costs on to the borrower, either because of statutory regulations or due to the borrower's economic situation, attempting to recover loans that are in arrears does not make economic sense. Thus, it is unlikely that the bank will take steps to enforce its claims, which gives the borrower an incentive not to pay back the loan (see also the theoretical derivation in Part I). High foreclosure and liquidation costs thus effectively preclude the development of a successful small-scale lending business.

In this section, three approaches are presented which can reduce the costs of enforcing claims. Firstly, statutory regulations can be amended so that the process of taking legal action to recover loans is less time-consuming and expensive. In the second concept, appliances or other goods used in the borrower's household are pledged as security, but without actually being pawned, i.e. without being physically delivered to the lender for safekeeping. The third procedure, developed in Uganda, involves the use of post-dated checks as collateral.

It should be noted that, regardless of the approach used to reduce foreclosure and liquidation costs, the bank could incur additional expenses if a borrower whose loan is overdue "disappears" and must first be found before steps can be taken to enforce the claim; however, these costs are not discussed, as they are similar to those generated by legal action to collect overdue loans. However, it should be clear that if claims are to be successfully enforced, the lender must be able to locate the delinquent borrower, and the costs generated by the search must not be prohibitively high. The "search costs" are affected by factors such as the efficiency of the country's registration system and its ability to provide current data on the whereabouts of all citizens and residents, as well as the mobility of borrowers.

In many countries, the laws currently on the books offer borrowers a very high degree of protection against the legal enforcement of claims arising from a loan, which of course drives up the costs of enforcing claims. In many cases, it is even unclear whether the court will "sentence" a delinquent borrower to the "punishment" of having to repay his loan. The ramifications of legal constraints of this type were described in Part I of the present study.

From an economic perspective, the easiest way of reducing the costs of foreclosing and liquidating collateral is no doubt to simplify the procedures involved in recovering overdue loans through legal action and to reduce the costs associated with such action. If this is done, it should be possible to have a court of law determine that a delinquent borrower is in arrears on the basis of nothing more than the existing loan agreement and the receipts issued for payments which have already been made, and then to have the courts and other state agencies enforce the lender's claims, i.e. foreclose and liquidate collateral, quickly and at a reasonable cost. From a technical standpoint this is not a particularly difficult task – it is enough to amend or simplify certain laws, and to ensure that the courts and the police have the resources needed to enforce the law.

However, the problem is that in many countries such measures are not politically feasible because borrowers incapable of repaying their loans are regarded as "victims" rather than legally competent adults who are fully responsible for the consequences of their actions. Because it is difficult to distinguish between the inability and the unwillingness to pay, public opinion tends to take the part of the borrowers, who are perceived as weak, rather than side with the banks, which are seen as strong, and indeed often regarded as omnipotent. Nonetheless, wherever possible, regulations which provide an excessive amount of protection to borrowers should be repealed. A more efficient financial market will surely do more to help the poor than the retention of laws which may occasionally serve to protect debtors against what could be seen as unfair loan recovery efforts, but which usually act as a deterrent to the enforcement by creditors of their just claims against delinquent borrowers.

Individual financial institutions are rarely able to influence legal regulations, and thus must adapt to them as part of the overall environment in which they operate. Consequently, institutions which successfully engage in small-scale lending have developed other instruments to enforce their claims which are appropriate to their situation and to that of their borrowers. One approach which has so far been very successful – and which would be suitable for most countries – requires borrowers to pledge personal property such as a television or refrigerator as security, but without delivering their collateral to the lender for safekeeping upon disbursement of the loan. Thus, the items remain in the possession of the borrower, and are seized by the bank only if overdue payments have been outstanding for more than a certain, predetermined length of time. In selecting the possessions to be pledged, the bank will be interested less in ensuring that the market value of the collateral fully covers the loan amount than in seeing to it that items are pledged whose seizure would have the greatest possible impact on the borrower's private life. The threat of losing the high utility value of a refrigerator or the "social status" of being able to watch television is a far more effective incentive to pay than could be created by having a borrower pledge other types of tangible assets which the borrower would not miss as much and which could be recovered by the borrower at a later time when it was more convenient for him to "divert" funds to meet his obligations to the lender. A reduction in the quality of his life is a greater punishment than temporarily having to give up the possession of property which, despite its higher value, is relatively easy to do without over the short term.

CERUDEB, a financial institution in Uganda, has developed and successfully implemented another instrument for enforcing claims. Use of this instrument was made possible by a new Cheques Law which makes issuing bad cheques a crime and threatens the "perpetrator" with immediate incarceration. Because the conditions in Uganda's prisons are, to say the least, unpleasant, the number of bad cheques issued has dropped dramatically since the law was passed.

CERUDEB has turned this new law to its advantage by having all borrowers sign a post-dated cheque in the amount of each instalment that will come due on their loans. After loan officers explain this clause of the institution's standard loan agreement, many borrowers decide not to sign, thus leading credit staff to suspect that they had the hidden intention of not repaying the loan. A few borrowers have decided to "call the institution's bluff", refusing to pay their instalments when they were due. They were promptly arrested, which, however, caused their relatives to settle their outstanding debts on their behalf. On the whole, the arrears rate has dropped considerably thanks to the new system.

Unlike the system involving pledged personal goods described above, this system is not suited to every environment. One precondition for its successful employment is that there must be a strict cheque law on the books which provides for the prosecution and relatively severe punishment of all persons who write bad cheques. On the other hand, however, the financial institution must also be capable of distinguishing between the inability to pay and the unwillingness to pay, for otherwise the system will in fact "produce victims", turning small-scale lending into something which is more likely to impede rather than promote the process of economic development.

d) How a reduction in the costs of enforcing claims affects lending practices

In this section, we will discuss how reducing the costs of enforcing claims will impact on the lending activities of banks. Because credit institutions base their calculations on average costs, the analysis is valid not only for a reduction in the costs of foreclosing and liquidating collateral, but also for an increase in the willingness to pay which results from the application of peer pressure, or from an increase in the bank's social proximity to its borrowers. For the sake of simplicity, however, our line of reasoning will refer only to "a reduction in the costs of foreclosing and liquidating collateral". Moreover, an empirical discussion of the effects of reduced claim-enforcement costs will not be presented because, as mentioned above, the favourable results achieved by successful institutions in practice are always attributable to the use of a balanced "mix" of measures.

Figure 29 shows how a reduction in the costs of foreclosing and liquidating collateral will affect the lending policies of banks, assuming that, as in the scenario described in Part I, the costs of enforcing claims are high and constitute a binding constraint, thus allowing banks to lend only to enterprises at least as large as $SE^{*\,min}_{for}$. Once costs have been reduced, borrowers' willingness to pay will be such that lending to enterprises as small as $SE^{*'\,min}_{for}$ would be permitted. However, the ability to pay, which thus constitutes the binding constraint in the example shown here, must also be taken into account, and thus the range of enterprises which are eligible for loans can only be extended downward as far as

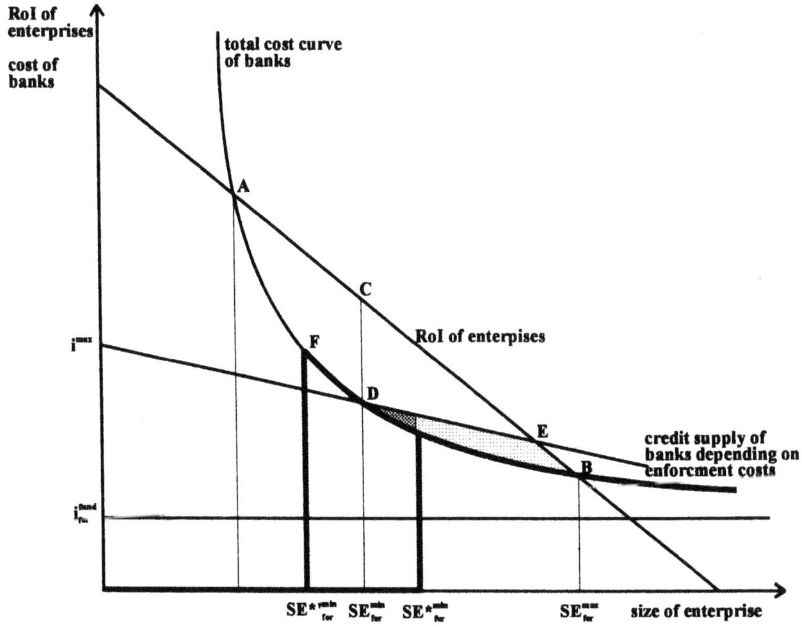

Fig. 29: How a reduction in the costs of foreclosing and liquidating collateral will affect the lending decisions taken by the banks

SE^{min}_{for}. Smaller enterprises will continue to be subject to rationing, although now for reasons related to asymmetric information. The contract area increases by the area shaded in dark grey.

On the basis of the scenario presented here, it is clear that it is very important to employ a balanced combination of various measures. For example, if the reduction in the costs of foreclosing and liquidating collateral is accompanied by a reduction in the extent of information problems, the drop in the costs of enforcing claims will have a much greater impact and the extent of credit rationing will be reduced further – indeed, all enterprises with a size of at least $SE^{*'min}_{for}$ will be eligible to borrow.

5. Institutional alternatives for small-scale lending

In the preceding chapters, various instruments were discussed, each which can enhance the efficiency of small-scale lending in certain ways. A characteristic of successful small loan programmes is that they employ a judicious mix of several of these tools, avoiding unnecessary costs by dispensing with instruments which are not essential to their strategy. In terms of the specific way in which they are organised, the majority of the world's successful small-scale lending programmes use one of three basic approaches – namely, the establishment of group credit programmes, the establishment of individual credit programmes, and the initiation of small-scale lending by existing banks. From an institution-building perspective, the first two options fall under the broad heading of "upgrading", while the third has come to be known as "downscaling". The present chapter is devoted to an analysis of these three approaches.

a) Basic design and mode of operation of group credit programmes

Approaches based on group lending have been very well known, and are very popular, among practitioners of development finance in many countries for a number of years. Credit extension based on borrower groups first began to be regarded as a viable strategy after the Grameen Bank in Bangladesh became the first target group oriented lending institution to demonstrate convincingly to knowledgeable observers that small-scale lending to the poor does not have to go hand-in-hand with high default rates. Owing to its rapid, widely publicised success, the Grameen Bank's concept has often been copied, and today is probably the most extensively used model for small-scale lending.

The objective of group credit programmes is to help combat poverty by eliminating as many factors as possible which serve to perpetuate a "culture of poverty". In other words, the range of services offered by group credit programmes usually include more than just financial services. Consequently, they are aimed at the poorest of the poor, i.e. the unemployed or the underemployed, who often have never had any occupational training or work experience whatsoever. Many group credit programmes lend exclusively to women.

To begin the lending process, loan officers recruit potential borrowers whose income and the amount of property they own may not exceed a given limit. These people attend a course for one to two weeks (usually in half-day sessions), in part to learn about all matters which are important for the future credit relationship, but also to establish personal relationships with the loan officer and (if necessary) with the other group members. In addition to successfully completing their training course, candidates must also exhibit sufficient discipline and have the personal qualities and attributes deemed to be necessary for participation in a group lending scheme. If they fulfil all of these requirements, they are admitted to the programme (screening) and organised into groups, which comprise between 5 and 30 members, depending on the institution.

Each group member submits a loan application which explains in detail how he or she intends to use the borrowed funds. The other group members are given the task of ensuring that the loan is in fact used as intended (peer monitoring). In order to ensure that group members have an economic incentive to actually perform this function, not all borrowers receive their loans immediately. The disbursement of funds to the remaining group members is contingent on whether the initial recipients pay their first instalments on time. It is important for such programmes to ensure that the use of the money is monitored, as the group members usually do not have capital of their own, and thus will only be able to pay back the loans if they invest the funds in some sort of productive economic activity (as opposed to using them to finance consumption of one sort or another).

The group meets once a week so that members can make payments and discuss group-related matters; meetings typically last one to two hours. Attendance is mandatory, and members are exempt only in exceptional cases and with good reason (e.g. pregnancy). Only those customers who pay on time *and* attend meetings on a regular basis are eligible for further loans.

If a borrower is late with a payment, it is the task of the other group members to induce him or her to pay by bringing social pressure to bear (peer pressure).

Social pressure can be a highly effective means of ensuring the willingness to pay. But if peer pressure is to work, two conditions must be met: on the one hand, the relationship between the borrowers must be characterised by a high degree of social proximity, so that disregard for the interests of the other members of the group has specific, tangible consequences. On the other hand, the group must be capable of assessing delinquent borrowers' actual ability to pay. If they cannot, borrowers who are willing but truly unable to pay, and who are ostracised because they are seen as having "refused to pay", will endure social hardships undeservedly.

The use of peer monitoring and peer pressure is grounded in the assumption that the information about the financial situation of group members needed to monitor repayment discipline and persuade borrowers who are in arrears to meet their obligations is already available (at no cost) to the other persons in the group, whereas the bank would first have to procure such information it were to assume these functions. Thus, instead of attempting to eliminate the asymmetric distribution of information between customer and bank, these approaches employ the other group members as agents who have a "competitive advantage" with respect to the bank, and thus can perform such activities at lower cost. If this is in fact the case, transferring responsibility for these tasks to the group members should serve to reduce the overall costs, i.e. all costs incurred by the banks and the borrowers.

However, peer monitoring can only be effective if the group members are capable of assessing each other's situation. This is especially likely to be the case in stable, rural regions, where the inhabitants know each other quite well and the requisite information will in fact be available at no cost. If the group is more or less homogenous in social and economic terms, they will be able to assess each other's ability to pay relatively easily; however, the greater the disparity between the economic situation of the individual members, the more difficult it will be for them to judge the others' capacity to pay. For this reason, group credit programmes establish relatively low maximum loan amounts.

Group credit programmes also create intertemporal incentives to give borrowers a further reason to want to pay back loans on time. Borrowers who pay all of their instalments on time and miss no more than one group meeting without an acceptable excuse are guaranteed a larger subsequent loan. In some cases, the increase in the size of the loan is contingent on provision of proof that the equity capital of the micro enterprise has increased by a certain minimum amount. As a rule, a borrower who was late in making one payment or who missed two or three group meetings is offered a follow-on loan of the same size as his or her first loan. However, intertemporal incentives become less effective once a borrower has become eligible to receive a loan for the maximum permissible amount, but this loss of effectiveness is compensated for by the intrinsic motivation to repay loans which borrowers will have developed by the time they reach this stage.

By combining peer monitoring, peer pressure and intertemporal incentives, successful group credit programmes have been able to keep their loan loss rates below 2 percent. Because responsibility for certain of the bank's tasks (monitoring and the enforcement of claims) is transferred to the borrowers, a satisfactory level of productivity can be achieved fairly quickly; in a successful group credit programme, each loan officer serves between 250 and 400 borrowers. In addition, the fact that they are geared to combating poverty enables group credit programmes to appeal to the "social conscience" of their employees and attract persons who are motivated at least in part by altruistic considerations. Thus, such programmes are able to hire qualified personnel despite the fact that they pay relatively low salaries. As a result, administration costs amount to only around 10%-20% of the loan portfolio.[57]

The terms and conditions of the loans tend to be very inflexible. Loan amounts are based on a fixed plan, to which there are no exceptions, i.e. the amount of the first loan is the same for all borrowers. The exact size of subsequent loans is also determined beforehand, and is not adjusted to take into account borrowers' needs or the economic development of their businesses. As a rule, all loans have a standard maturity of one year. While this type of rigid system obviously lowers costs and does not require the banks to invest much in the development of institutional capacity, it also renders the loans less valuable to the customers.

The costs for the borrowers comprise manifest, hidden, and non-monetary components. Manifest costs include interest and fees, which in real terms usually work out to 15%-35% of the loan amount. Borrowers must also bear hidden costs because nearly all group credit programmes involve mandatory savings schemes: At each weekly meeting, every member of the borrower group is required to deposit a certain amount of money in a savings account, and these funds cannot be withdrawn until he or she leaves the programme.

Of course, these savings deposits bear interest at a lower rate than that charged on the loans. At the same time, mandatory savings boost the customers' credit requirements, as the funds tied up in savings cannot be used for investments. Consequently, this involves an extension of the borrower's balance sheet, i.e. a rise on both the liability and the asset side equal to the amount of the

[57] See, for example, JAIN, 1997, p.12, p. 29.

savings deposits, which causes the borrowers to incur costs equal to the difference between the interest rate earned on deposits and the rate charged on loans. These costs must be added to the manifest costs of credit.

Finally, the non-monetary credit costs must be considered: The borrowers must take time to attend group meetings each week, which is time they could have spent working. Although they do not have to pay to attend the meetings, being present nonetheless implies a loss of income, and the opportunity costs of their labour must therefore be used to measure the precise extent of this loss. The same is true of the time they spend attending the training course.

Assessing the impact of these opportunity costs is not as simple as might seem at first glance. We must first determine how high the opportunity costs of the borrowers' labour are. If the borrowers are established micro entrepreneurs, forgone income must be factored into the calculation because the opportunity costs for this group of customers are relatively high. However, group credit programmes are typically aimed at the unemployed or at highly underemployed persons, for whom the opportunity costs of labour are initially close to zero. Of course, if these customers succeed in using their loans to establish viable micro enterprises, the opportunity costs of their labour will increase steadily over time.

The training phase and the group meetings can also be helpful to the customers. While established micro entrepreneurs will derive little or no real benefit from participation in these aspects of the group credit programme, they offer the members of the typical target group an opportunity to acquire, for the first time, a modicum of self-confidence and discipline – qualities without which they would not be able to operate a business successfully in the first place. The regular group meetings serve as a forum for sharing experiences, and thus at the beginning are very useful, although their usefulness to the borrowers decreases with the passage of time.

Initially, the amounts tied up in mandatory savings are minimal and therefore generate only minimal costs for the borrowers. In return for the costs they incur, the borrowers receive valuable "insurance benefits". For example, when individual group members suffer a personal financial catastrophe such as can be brought on by the illness or death of a family member, their hardship can be eased with emergency loans funded by the group's savings; in many cases these loans save borrowers from total economic ruin. However, the value of these "insurance services" remains constant over time, whereas the value of savings – and thus the level of costs resulting from the interest rate differential – increases steadily. These higher costs are initially compensated by increasing loan amounts; however, after a borrower has become eligible for the maximum loan amount, the costs generated by the interest rate differential continue to rise, whereas the value of the credit and the insurance remains constant. Indeed, for credit customers who have been with the programme for many years, the amount of their savings deposits often exceeds the size of their loans. Thus, they are net savers who must nonetheless pay interest to obtain part of "their" funds.

On the whole, then, the hidden and non-monetary costs of credit increase over time, while the value of the benefits the borrowers can receive in exchange for these costs decreases. In particular, customers who have taken part in the programme for a number of years are at a disadvantage because they find that the financial services offered are no longer appropriate to their needs, given the way their enterprises have grown and developed. In addition to greater flexibility with respect to loan amounts and payment schedules, a more appropriate range of services would include the option of applying for parallel loans to meet peak borrowing requirements, as well as other types of banking products such as payment services. While the spectrum of products offered by group credit programmes is well-suited to the needs of newly recruited customers from the ranks of the poorest of the poor, successful micro entrepreneurs "outgrow" these institutions, as they do not provide services which are tailored to these borrowers' evolving, more sophisticated requirements. Indeed, it has been observed that in cases where group and individual credit programmes compete with one another, many successful, long-time customers of group credit programmes (must) switch to the individual programmes in order to meet their need for banking services.[58]

Group credit programmes have competitive advantages vis-à-vis individual loan programmes when it comes to serving extremely poor segments of the population. They are the only programmes which are capable not only of providing poor people with loans, but also of boosting their self-respect and discipline – qualities which self-employed persons must possess if they are to have any chance of success. As a consequence, they are in a position to help the poorest of the poor to escape from the confines of economic marginalisation. It is in this way that group credit programmes have probably contributed most to fighting poverty.

Because the terms and conditions of group loans are extremely rigid, group credit programmes can operate without sophisticated institutional structures, and their employees also do not have to meet very high standards as regards their professional qualifications and training. The other side of the coin, however, is that the resulting limitations in effect leave successful customers with no choice but to switch to other providers. Thus, group credit programmes which are not

58 See, for example, BancoSol and Caja de los Andes in Bolivia.

supplemented by individual credit programmes can alleviate poverty, but not eliminate it.

b) Basic design and mode of operation of individual credit programmes

Individual credit programmes pursue the goal of deepening the financial market, i.e. they are geared to granting formal-sector loans to borrowers who previously had to rely on informal credit. These programmes seek to establish sustainable financial institutions, which implies that the revenue obtained from lending must at least be sufficient to cover the costs it generates. Consequently, potential customers and market segments which would be particularly difficult to serve on a cost-covering basis – e.g. persons who wish to start a new business, or those who demand extremely small loans – are not given access to loans on any appreciable scale. The target group of these institutions thus comprises established micro entrepreneurs with business experience whose opportunities for growth are to be enhanced through the provision of more affordable financing options.

In these programmes, it is not the task of the loan officers to recruit potential borrowers. Their work begins once persons have submitted a loan application to the institution. First of all, a cash-flow analysis is performed which takes into account the financial situation of the prospective borrower's entire family economic unit; i.e. comprehensive data on the income and expenditures of both the business and the household is compiled, and this information is used as the basis for assessing that customer's creditworthiness (screening). The repayment schedule is then tailored to the requirements of the family economic unit, i.e. designed so as to be compatible with its specific cash-flow pattern. This is meant to ensure the borrower's ability to pay even if his or her income does not increase as a result of the loan. At the same time, the informational asymmetry is eliminated, or even reversed.

Monitoring takes place exclusively on the basis of the payment flows. In other words, the institution does not check up on its customers to ensure that they are using their loans as intended. In fact, this would not even be possible given the fungibility of money. As long as borrowers pay their instalments on time, the institution does not take any further action. However, if someone is late with a payment, this is noted immediately in the computer system, and during the next few days a loan officer will attempt to induce the borrower to meet his or her obligations. The institution will bring pressure to bear on the borrower by threatening to seize collateral pledged when the loan agreement was signed – usually household goods such as a television set or a refrigerator. Although these goods are returned when the bank receives the overdue payments, the borrower must do without them until the relevant payment has been made – a prospect which normally increases the willingness to pay to such an extent that borrowers give priority to meeting their obligations to the bank when deciding how to allocate available funds; their cash-flow usually gives them sufficient leeway to take this kind of decision.

Individual credit programmes also use intertemporal incentives to motivate borrowers to pay on time. Borrowers who on average are only slightly behind in their payments (e.g. less than three days for each instalment) are guaranteed access to future loans. However, an increase in the loan amount is contingent on a given borrower's economic situation, i.e. a larger loan amount will only be approved if a new cash-flow analysis reveals that his or her ability to pay has increased. Moreover, many institutions offer preferential loan terms to borrowers who have made their payments on time over an extended period.

However, there is also very little "value" in refusing to pay, as the institution is prepared to pursue all legal options to recover overdue payments. Because loans are disbursed only to established micro entrepreneurs, who generally use them to finance a relatively small portion of their assets (10%-20%), the bank is usually able to enforce its claims. Refusing to pay would have only negative repercussions for borrowers, and thus would be irrational.

Taken together, these measures enable successful individual credit programmes to limit their loan loss rates to less than one percent. In comparison with the credit technology used by group credit programmes, however, this approach makes much greater demands on the lender's institutional resources and capacity (e.g. in terms of its computer system) and presupposes the availability of much more highly qualified staff. But as a consequence, there is greater scope for efficiency gains as staff become more proficient at their jobs. Thus, while productivity tends to be relatively low in the initial phase of the programme (around 50-100 borrowers per loan officer), later on it begins to rise noticeably and keeps on increasing until a level similar to that achieved by group credit programmes (i.e. around 400 borrowers per loan officer) is reached (see Figure 30). However, because individual credit programmes tend to pay their employees salaries which are in line with current "market rates" of compensation, their administrative costs are, at 15%-30%, higher than those of group credit programmes.

In return for these higher costs, individual credit programmes are able to develop resources which enable them to adapt their services more closely to the needs of their customers. The size of loans is determined on the basis of the borrowers' credit requirements and/or their maximum payment capacity. Moreover, because loan officers can easily monitor larger loans, loan amounts can usually be increased as borrower's requirements increase.[59] The payment schedule is tailored to reflect the cash flow of each borrower's family economic unit.

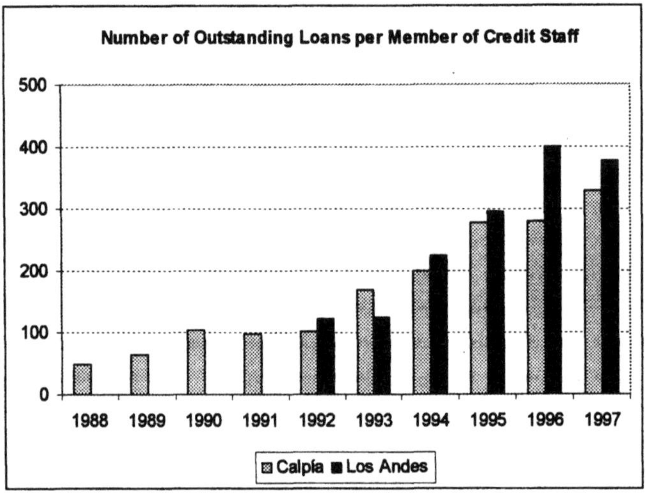

Fig. 30: Examples of how the productivity of individual credit programmes develops over time, based on data provided by Calpiá and Caja de los Andes
Source: Lepp, 1997, p. 3

The real interest rate on individual loans usually ranges between 20% and 40%, and thus is slightly higher than the rate charged on group loans. On the other hand, individual loans generate no hidden costs, as borrowers are not required to maintain savings deposits at the institution in order to be eligible for credits. Moreover, the non-monetary costs are low, at least in urban areas, because customers need only wait a few minutes at the teller's window to conduct their payment transactions. In rural regions, though, travel expenses and time must also be factored in, as staff of individual credit programmes usually do not come to customers' villages to collect instalments. As a consequence, the

[59] Of course, this applies only so long as the customer does not wish to borrow more than the maximum loan amount stipulated by the institution. However, it takes "new customers" a long time to reach this point, and it is usually not a problem for borrowers who have "outgrown" the maximum loan size to find another bank which will meet their financing requirements.

competitive advantage of these institutions over group lending programmes is greater in urban areas than in rural regions.

The credit technology used by individual loan programmes does not allow for the provision of an integrated package of credit and (mandatory) savings services, which also means that they cannot offer their customers a means of accumulating financial reserves as a kind of insurance for emergencies. In other words, although there are no hidden credit costs, individual borrowers are also unable to take advantage of any of the additional benefits typically provided by group credit programmes. We demonstrated above that as borrowers attain higher levels of economic development, the value of these additional benefits declines more and more while the cost of obtaining them, i.e. the cost of the "insurance service", increases. Thus, individual loans are of particular interest for borrowers who have already achieved a somewhat higher level of economic development. This segment of the market, i.e. established small and micro entrepreneurs, is in any case the target group of these institutions, and as a result the range of products they offer is well-tailored to the requirements of this clientele.

Individual credit programmes help to combat poverty by providing their customers with credit which is much less expensive than informal-sector loans. They boost borrowers' income by the difference in the amount of interest paid on loans granted by individual credit programmes and that paid on informal sector loans. Moreover, individual loan programmes also eliminate obstacles to growth (see Part I), and, by fostering the growth of small and micro enterprises, they help to create jobs in these businesses for poor people who were previously unemployed or underemployed, which in turn indirectly increases their (earned) income.

Individual credit programmes thus help the poorest of the poor only indirectly, but nonetheless at least eliminate one of the structural causes of poverty. Over the long term, they will probably do more to actually combat poverty than group credit programmes, which can only alleviate its effects.

c) Downscaling the lending activities of banks

A third institutional alternative for small-scale lending is to "downscale" the lending activities of banks. Rather than setting up a new institution, this approach instead makes it economically advantageous for existing institutions to grant small loans to the target group. For the most part, downscaling programmes use the same credit technology as individual credit programmes; for this reason, the credit technology will not be described again here. Instead, the following discussion will focus on the institutional differences between downscaling and the creation of new, target group-oriented institutions.

Banks are profit-oriented institutions. Thus, they will only be prepared to grant small loans if they can expect that such activities will increase their overall earnings. To determine if this condition will in fact be met, the operating result which a given bank can expect to achieve in its small-scale lending business must be weighed against the external effects of this activity on its other operations.

In particular, one consideration is that regular customers might take their business elsewhere if they see "hundreds of ragged, poor micro entrepreneurs" making loan payments at the same branches they frequent. Such negative external effects of small-scale lending can naturally be avoided if the bank opens up separate branches for this type of business. However, the particular appeal of the downscaling approach is that existing banks which seek to initiate micro lending activities can make use of an extensive, established branch network; if the bank first had to invest in setting up new facilities, downscaling would be a less appealing option.

Because banks do not choose to enter the small-scale lending business, it can be assumed that they do not consider it worthwhile to develop this segment of the market. If one nevertheless wishes to persuade them to grant small loans, one must make them an attractive offer entailing the provision of certain subsidies. These subsidy components must not only make small-scale lending less expensive and more profitable; in addition, they must, if at all possible, induce positive external effects which will make the banks more competitive in their core businesses.

The costs of small-scale lending can be reduced by using the credit technology described in the preceding section. However, this technology is so different from the banks' conventional lending methodology that introducing it would give rise to considerable costs which they would be reluctant to assume. Thus, downscaling projects should contain a subsidy component which makes resources available to train staff members in the use of the new technology and create the necessary institutional capacity (funding for the start-up phase). As the banks acquire more and more experience in small-scale lending and become increasingly proficient at serving the target group, they will also be able reap ever greater economies of scale, causing their costs to drop over time.

In particular, the income generated by small-scale lending can be increased by permitting the disbursement of somewhat larger loans, which of course are more profitable than loans at the lower end of the "small and micro" size range. An interest rate ceiling should not be set. Instead, competition in this market segment should be increased by offering several banks the same assistance simultaneously. If small-scale lending proves to be a truly profitable activity for the banks, they will begin on their own to take steps to boost their market share, offering customers more favourable terms and conditions and granting increasingly smaller loans.

Finally, offering the banks long-term loans (at market interest rates) to fund their small-scale lending activities will have positive external effects on their main lines of business. As donor organisations have access to long-term loans on the international markets, they can readily provide long-term credit facilities to banks which have decided to begin serving small and micro enterprises. Especially for smaller banks in "developing countries", access to facilities of this type is highly advantageous, as they themselves cannot obtain long-term financing in the international markets. Provision of long-term funding for (short-term) small loans enables such banks to achieve a *negative* maturity transformation in this area, which in turn allows them to undertake an meaningful internal reallocation of resources: they grant small and micro loans using the plentiful supply of short-term funds at their disposal (short-term liabilities), while using the long-term credit lines provided by donor organisations to fund large, long-term loans, which are more profitable.

While the downscaling approach appears to be simple and attractive in theory, it is difficult to implement successfully in practice. The banks have strong incentives to find ways of simply "pocketing" the subsidies without making a serious commitment to small-scale lending. For example, in order to qualify for assistance they can, for the purposes of a downscaling programme, claim to have issued small loans to informal entrepreneurs, when in fact they have granted consumer loans to salaried employees in the formal sector; or they might obtain resources from donor organisations to pay for small and micro loan officer training measures and then use these employees in other areas of their business. If the banks are able to "misappropriate" the subsidies intended to promote the introduction of small and micro lending, these funds will in effect have been wasted as they will not have contributed to the desired deepening of the financial market. However, it is difficult – and often prohibitively expensive – to effectively monitor the use of such funds by the banks.

For these reasons, downscaling is especially attractive if competition in the financial market of a country increases, thereby squeezing the banks' profit margins. In a situation like this, at least some banks will be forced to look for new market niches, which in turn means that a move into the small and micro enterprise credit market can be prove to be a successful strategy. If it turns out that this market segment can be served profitably, other banks will follow suit.

Part IV. Impact Analysis of Small Loan Programmes

In Part III, we examined several instruments to assess their ability to eliminate, or at least alleviate, the problems described in the first two parts of this study. Part IV will analyse how the economic environment is affected when small-scale lending activities are rendered more efficient. Chapter 1 examines the impacts of increased efficiency on the functioning of the financial markets and the size distribution of enterprises – impacts which are a function of the extent to which efficiency is raised. Chapter 2 analyses how the labour market and the sectoral distribution of economic activity are influenced. Next, Chapter 3 shows how enhanced efficiency in lending impacts the income of various groups, namely the borrowers themselves, "non-borrowers" and consumers. Finally, in Chapter 4 the focus shifts to the economy as a whole, and possible effects at the macro level are described.

1. Impacts on the financial market and the size distribution of enterprises

This chapter examines how the financial sector is affected when small-scale lending becomes more efficient. The long-term objective of every development strategy should always be to help people to help themselves, i.e. improve their situation by their own efforts. In the context of small-scale lending, this means that small-scale borrowers should finally become an attractive market segment, and that profit-oriented financial intermediaries should offer services to this group because it is in their own best interests to do so – in other words, because catering to their demand is a profitable undertaking. In Part III, instruments were discussed which render small-scale lending a more attractive line of business for financial institutions. Thus far, though, we have not explored the question of just how pronounced the impact of these instruments must be before financial intermediaries will actually begin offering small loans of their own accord. Moreover, we have not yet discussed strategies which would ensure that small loans will be granted even if, from the point of view of an institution that is exclusively profit-oriented, small-scale lending is not a (fully) commercially viable activity.

As was the case in Part I, the following analysis begins by applying the Stiglitz-Weiss model. In other words, it distinguishes between only two groups of borrowers – those who demand "large" loans, and those who demand "small" loans. Next, the results of this initial phase of the analysis will be transposed onto a continuum of possible loan sizes using the basic model, which will enable us to infer how improvements in the efficiency of small-scale lending would affect the size distribution of enterprises.

a) The Stiglitz-Weiss model

Depending on the extent to which the efficiency of lending is enhanced, the financial market will be affected in a variety of ways. Four different scenarios are presented below, with the results and consequences derived for each.

Small-scale lending as a product of market forces

In competitive markets, services are offered if they can be expected to generate a higher return than could be achieved by investing in alternative projects. However, if a market is not fully competitive – as is assumed to be the case in most "developing countries" – the analysis must take other factors into consideration. With respect to small and micro lending in particular, one must bear in mind that:

a) a bank which begins offering micro and small loans may become less attractive to its existing customers, perhaps because the latter wish to avoid any contact whatsoever with small or micro entrepreneurs,

b) the bank managers themselves have reservations regarding this group of customers, or

c) the social distance between the bank and the target group is so great that bank staff cannot accurately assess the situation of small and micro entrepreneurs, and thus they regard them as "unknown quantities" who must be assumed to be bad credit risks.

The more pronounced these obstacles are, the more the expected return on small-scale lending must exceed the return on "large loans". However, it is also possible that public opinion will put pressure on the banks to grant small loans, and that offering these services will enhance the banks' reputation, thus making them more attractive to potential customers. As a result, they will be willing to grant small loans even if the expected return on such credits is lower than that generated by large loans.[60]

---

60 As a rule, though, public opinion also insists that the interest rates on small loans should be in the same general range as those charged on large loans. This not only makes it impossible for the banks to earn an acceptable return; in fact, it ensures that they will lose money on this line of business.

Figure 31 depicts these relationships in a form compatible with the Stiglitz-Weiss model. For large loans, there is a correlation between the interest rate and the bank's return which corresponds to the function $r(i)^{large}_{gross}$, or, after deducting transaction costs, $r(i)^{large}_{net}$. In conventional small-scale lending using standard credit technologies, which is represented by the broken lines, the maximum return which banks can earn on small loans – r^{max}_{small} – is substantially lower than the return on large loans (r^{max}_{large}).

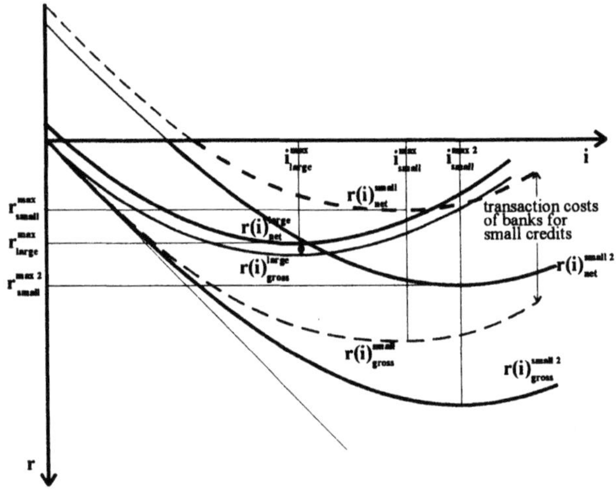

Fig. 31: Small-scale lending as a product of market forces

We will now assume that a more efficient credit technology is introduced for small-scale lending which not only limits the risks (flattens and extends the function $r(i)^{small}_{gross}$) but also lowers the transaction costs (reduces the distance between the gross and net return). The result is the net return function $r(i)^{small\,2}_{net}$. In other words, the maximum return on small-scale lending increases to $r^{max\,2}_{small}$, and is thus higher than the return on large loans. Therefore, the banks now have an economic incentive to grant small loans. Even if they have reason to fear that becoming involved in small-scale lending will have a negative impact on their established large-scale lending activities, in a market which is at least somewhat competitive there will usually be at least one bank that will choose to specialise in small-scale lending, perhaps abandoning its traditional lines of business in the process. The high return on small-scale lending enables this bank to grow rapidly, which not only ensures that the target group will have access to credit, but also demonstrates to other banks that catering to the demand in this market segment can in fact be profitable. Over the medium to long term, an increasing number of institutions will begin serving this part of the market, and the resulting competition will cause banks to offer borrowers increasingly favourable terms and conditions on small-scale loans.

Is this scenario too optimistic? Possibly, although there is good evidence that it is basically realistic. Experience has shown that as banks become more proficient at small-scale lending, their productivity increases substantially, which over the long term lowers costs. In Peru, for example, municipal savings banks which were established as part of an upgrading project have been offering financial services to small and micro entrepreneurs for over a decade, and in the meantime are earning substantial profits. This has not escaped the notice of other financial intermediaries; in particular, the Chilean *financieras* that have been moving into the Peruvian market on an increasing scale in recent years, have already recognised that small-scale lending can be a profitable business. However, they focus exclusively on the most profitable and least complicated part of this market, namely the provision of "consumer loans" to salaried employees in the formal sector. It should be noted, though, that a considerable share of these loans (around 30%) are passed on to family members who use them to finance the operations of a micro enterprise.

As a result of the Chilean *financieras* entering the market, the credit supply for micro entrepreneurs has expanded considerably, even though the latter benefit only indirectly from the increased availability of small loans. One drawback of this "arrangement", however, is that micro entrepreneurs only have access to credit if one of their family members is a salaried employee in the formal sector. In terms of its income-related effects, an approach to small-scale lending that addresses only a portion of the overall target group of small and micro entrepreneurs will have mixed benefits, as will be shown in Section IV.3.a.

Small-scale lending as a product of externally induced economic incentives

In most "developing countries", small-scale lending is not as profitable as granting large loans. This situation is depicted in Figure 32, which shows only the net return functions that obtain following the introduction of the new credit technologies. If, as a result of the demand for large loans, the interest rate on such loans is higher than i_{large}^{crit}, the banks will not offer small loans at all. Even given an interest rate of just under i_{large}^{crit}, the banks will not be willing to make an investment in what for them is a new credit technology. Moreover, in this case the size of the supply of small loans would in large part be a function of fluctuations in demand in the market for large loans, and thus access to small loans would not be guaranteed over the long term (see also Part I).

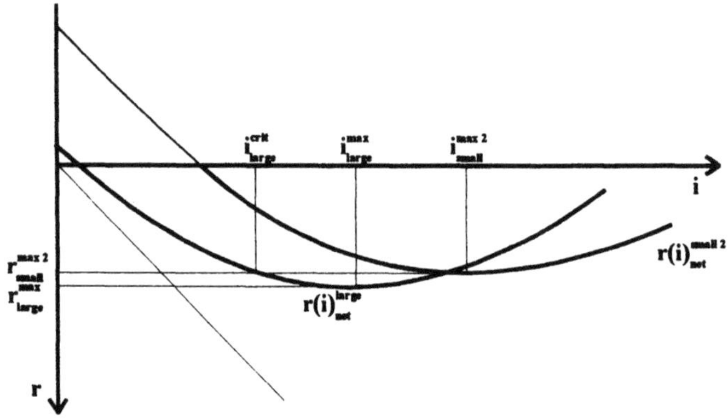

Fig. 32: Small-scale lending as a product of externally induced economic incentives

Therefore, in the case shown here, a profit-oriented bank will as a rule not grant small loans because the expected return on large loans – which do not require additional investments on its part – is the same or (slightly) higher.

However, if one nonetheless wishes to convince the banks to grant small loans, one must offer them economic incentives which will increase the expected return on small-scale lending to such an extent that it becomes worthwhile for them to take up this line of business (see III.5.c). The "Micro-Global" programmes which the Inter-American Development Bank (IDB) has implemented in a number of Latin American countries are an example of this approach. These programmes are based on a concept in which the IDB subsidises the costs arising from the introduction of a new credit technology by providing the banks with technical assistance at no cost to them. In addition, through a rediscount mechanism, the banks are entitled to receive long-term loans from the IDB equivalent to the size of their small loan portfolio. Even though the rates paid by the banks on these funds are in line with the prevailing money market rate, such an option is nonetheless very attractive for them because they have scarcely any long-term deposits, and would thus be exposed to an extremely high level of risk if they were to issue long-term loans.

Given their access to the IDB funds, banks engaging in small-scale lending are able to achieve a negative maturity transformation, i.e. short-term loans are funded with long-term borrowings. This in turn enables the institutions to restructure their portfolios by funding short-term small loans with short-term resources (deposits), of which they have an abundant supply. On the other hand, the long-term funds provided by the Inter-American Development Bank are used to issue large loans with long maturities, which are highly profitable. The sizeable profits they generate are more than sufficient to offset the (presumably rather small) losses incurred in small-scale lending.

The advantage of this approach from the point of view of the Inter-American Development Bank is that a relatively large supply of small loans can be created at relatively low cost in a short period of time. And because the banks are only eligible to borrow an amount equivalent to the size of their small-loan portfolios, the IDB is also able to ensure that small borrowers will not lose their access to credit during the next cyclical increase in the demand for large loans.

Small-scale lending as a product of the establishment of new, target group-oriented financial institutions

Conceivably, the expected return on small loans will turn out to be much lower than what the banks can earn on large loans. If the banks consider small-scale lending to be much less profitable than large-scale lending, these are some of the factors that may be responsible for the sizeable differential:

a) Inefficient operating procedures or poorly trained personnel may have pushed up the costs incurred by the banks.

b) There may be subsidised small loan programmes in operation which, while offering only a small number of loans for micro entrepreneurs, provide credits at sufficiently low interest rates to make the higher, cost-covering interest rates charged by banks seem usurious to their customers. As a consequence, the willingness to pay decreases (moral hazard; hidden intention) and the loan default rate rises accordingly.

c) Owing to unfavourable overall economic conditions, micro entrepreneurs may be achieving a lower RoI than expected; if they are, their ability to pay will have decreased and the banks' default risk will have increased.

d) Highly unstable political or economic conditions causes borrowers' time horizons to shrink dramatically, with little no planning being done for the future; the value of future loans, and thus the willingness to pay, decreases.

e) Given the great social distance which separates them from small and micro entrepreneurs, bank staff may be unable to assess the probable repayment behaviour of potential customers from this target group. Because they do not really trust small borrowers, i.e. because bank staff think they are considerably less creditworthy than they in fact are, the expected return on small-scale lending is considerably lower than the return that would actually have been achieved had loans been granted.

Figure 33 is a graphic representation of a situation in which the expected return on small-scale lending ($r_{small}^{max\,2}$) is considerably lower than the return on large loans despite the use of an efficient credit technology. Thus, no bank will be willing to grant small loans. Owing to the large differential between the return on large loans and that generated by small loans, it would be too expensive to subsidise the banks' small-scale lending activities. Subsidies are thus not a feasible solution to the problem.

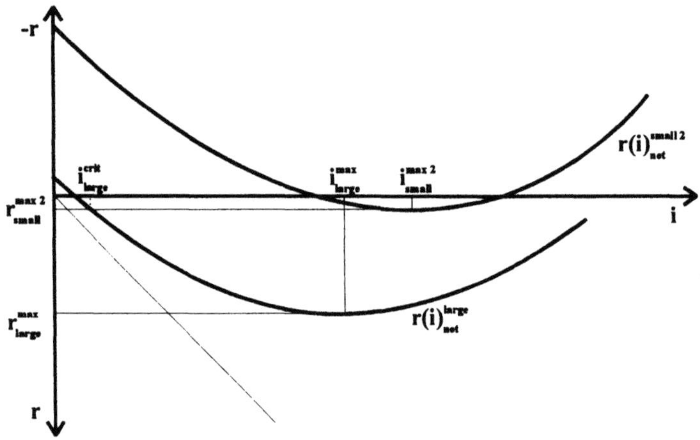

Fig. 33: Provision of small-scale loans by target group-oriented financial intermediaries

The creation of a new, target group-oriented financial institution can nonetheless stimulate the financial market in a way that induces formal institutions to grant small loans. In addition to furnishing extensive technical assistance to support the design and establishment of the institution and its operation during the start-up phase, development aid agencies provide the new intermediary with equity capital (at no cost), as well as soft loans (i.e. loans granted at below-market interest rates). Thus, given its very low funding costs, the new bank can cover the operating costs of its lending activities, even if its return comes to only r_{small}^{max2}. However, it is highly unlikely that achievement of cost coverage in this way, i.e. by utilising subsidised funding sources, will create a sufficiently strong "demonstration effect" to induce other banks to begin granting small loans to the target group.

All the same, in many cases it will become apparent that if an appropriate credit technology is used, the credit risks are far lower than the banks generally suppose; in other words, the banks' actual return will turn out to be substantially higher than their expected return.

Furthermore, one objective of the technical support should be to adapt the credit technology and the operating procedures to the particular situation of the country in question and to continue optimising them; if this is done, the costs of intermediation should decline further, enabling the banks to earn an even higher return.

These two effects of technical assistance are depicted in Figure 34. In addition to the bank's expected return (as illustrated in Fig. 33), the diagram shows the actual return ($r(i)^{actual}_{netto}$) as well as the even higher return resulting from improved efficiency ($r(i)^{incr}_{netto}$). In the latter case, a subsidy component could be implemented simultaneously in order to expand small-scale lending more quickly.

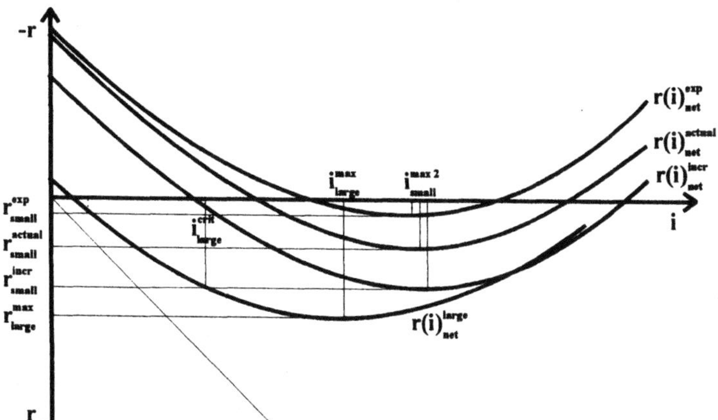

Fig. 34: Expected, actual and enhanced return on small-scale lending

The long-term goal of further developing and optimising small-scale lending via the new institution should be to increase the actual net return on small loans to such an extent that small-scale lending becomes more profitable than the provision of large loans. If it does, other banks will then serve the target group in a competitive market.

Solutions involving subsidies are primarily intended to introduce established credit technologies at the banks while providing funds to cover the gap between the return achievable on large loans and that generated by small loans – a differential will still exist even after more efficient lending methodologies have been adopted. By contrast, the establishment of new, target group-oriented intermediaries not only provides the target group with access to credit, but in addition supports the ongoing development and improvement of the small-scale lending technology and of the new institutions' operating procedures. Over time, this can reduce, or even eliminate altogether, the differential between the returns on large and small loans.

Small-scale lending as a social service

If, over the long term, small-scale lending generates a negative net return, then the activity involved here should not be referred to as "a subsidised small credit programme", but rather as "the provision of social services". A negative net return is often an outgrowth of the humanitarian desire to help the poor which informs the approach taken by many small credit programmes. Through their lending activities, such programmes seek above all to support the poorest of the poor, i.e. those members of the population who are most disadvantaged. Thus, they logically grant particularly small – and thus particularly cost-intensive – loans, while often neglecting, or even disdaining, operational efficiency and financial viability. Indeed, a study on the efficiency of financial NGOs in Latin America revealed that the administrative and risk-related costs of institutions that defined their mission as "helping the poor" were on average 50% higher than those of "market-oriented" NGOs.[61]

Of course, providing social services in the form of small loans can be a worthwhile undertaking. For this to be the case, however, the social impact of the subsidies employed must be greater than the effect which would be achieved by applying the funds in other ways, such as investing in schools or improved health care. In Section IV.3.b, the findings of a study will be presented which suggests that lending to the poorest of the poor does not meet this criterion.

---

61 Cf. SCHMIDT/ZEITINGER, 1996, p. 247.

b) The basic model

The results derived above using the STIGLITZ/WEISS model are based on the assumption that small loans are demanded and provided in only one (standard) size. However, this restriction is quite misleading. For example, if the lender has fixed administrative costs of $40 per loan, then given a maturity of one year, the administrative cost would be 40% of a loan for $200 but only 10% of a loan of $800.[62] The size of this differential underscores that, at a single point in time and in a single country, empirical examples could certainly be found which would demonstrate the validity of all of the scenarios described in the preceding section; one would need only consider a correspondingly large range of loan sizes. Thus, we will continue our analysis using the basic model, which can be used to derive the impacts of improvements in lending efficiency for small loans of various sizes. After the direct effects have been examined, possible longer-term consequences will be discussed.

Figure 35 shows the **direct effects** which the introduction of new credit technologies will have on the financial market (e.g. through a Micro-Global programme). Transaction costs decrease and information problems are alleviated, which causes a slight rotation of the maximum interest rate line and the cost curve for the banks (broken lines). The contract area increases by the area shaded in grey; in other words, banks are able to grant relatively large small loans that are demanded by enterprises larger than SE_{inf}^{max}. However, even following the introduction of a more efficient credit technology, loans at the lower end of the small-scale range are still too cost-intensive, and are thus not offered by the banks.

In this situation, credit market segmentation still exists, i.e. the interest rate differentials between the two sub-markets are not solely a function of varying loan sizes. For example, enterprises whose size corresponds to SE_{inf}^{max} can borrow either in the formal or the informal sector at widely divergent interest rates (F' or F). Even if efficiency were enhanced somewhat further, credit market segmentation would continue to exist until the formal financial sector was able to offer even the smallest enterprises that must rely on informal providers lower interest rates than they can obtain in the informal sector. However, this is not a goal which can realistically be achieved in the foreseeable future, and thus credit programmes should not even attempt to eliminate credit market segmentation altogether. Instead, the objective should be to ensure that the financial sector functions at least well enough to make it feasible to overcome long-term

62 For loans to be paid back in regular, uniform instalments.

impediments to growth such as the constraints faced by small enterprises that were derived in Part II.

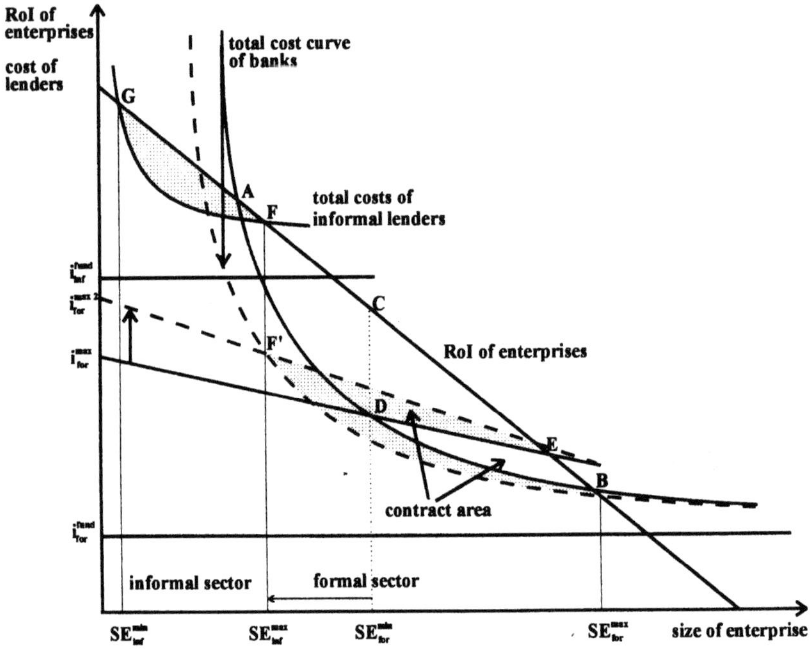

Fig. 35: The direct effects of the introduction of more efficient credit technologies on the credit market

Enhancing efficiency to the extent shown in the diagram will be just sufficient to close the credit gap between the formal and informal sectors of the credit market – in other words, every enterprise will now have access to credit in one of the two sub-markets. Despite the continued presence of credit market segmentation, the growth potential of small enterprises is no longer constrained by a lack of access to credit. Indeed, although the interest rate differential, which is represented by the segment FF', persists, it now gives enterprises an economic incentive to grow to an extent which will permit them to cross the critical size threshold represented by SE^{max}_{inf}. As a result, segmentation in the size distribution of enterprises will be eliminated over the long term.

However, it would be premature to end the analysis here. If these measures truly impact the credit market in the way described above, there will also be a number of **indirect effects**. Enterprises which now have access to the relatively inexpensive loans available in the formal financial sector, and therefore face lower costs, will take advantage of the situation by expanding their output. They are able to undertake such an expansion because, on the one hand, access to inexpensive credit enables them to operate at a higher level of capital intensity and augment their capacity without having to hire new personnel. On the other hand, it is relatively easy for them to sell their additional output at slightly reduced prices. Thus, owing to the decrease in costs, their overall RoI will decline only slightly or not at all. Competition will intensify.

However, the other enterprises which operate in the same market segment as businesses that are profiting from newly obtained access to formal sector credit will have to respond to the lowering of prices by the latter, i.e. they will be forced to lower their prices as well. However, as these enterprises' costs have not dropped, their RoI will decrease, which not only affects the income of the entrepreneurs in question, but also has repercussions for the credit market.

These factors have been taken into account in Figure 36. Formal-sector enterprises are affected by the situation described above only if goods produced in the informal sector provide at least an imperfect substitute for their own products. In the diagram, it is assumed that the products of very large enterprises cannot be substituted by informal-sector products; however, as the size of enterprise decreases, substitutability (and thus cross price elasticity) increases. As a consequence, the smaller the enterprise, the more its RoI will be adversely affected if competitors are able to lower their prices because access to formal sector credit has reduced their costs.

This decline in the RoI of enterprises has a direct impact on both the formal and informal financial sectors. In the formal financial sector the contract area is diminished because a drop in enterprises' RoI increases the risk-related costs borne by the banks and causes a slight downward rotation of the maximum interest rate line (i_{for}^{max3}). As a result, the minimum enterprise size for formal loans increases once again (from SE_{inf}^{max} to SE_{for}^{min3}).

The informal credit sector is affected to a much greater extent. Assuming that the costs incurred by informal providers remain constant, a lower RoI will cause the informal contract area to shrink considerably to the area shaded in black (KI), and a great many micro and small entrepreneurs will find that it is no longer profitable to finance business activities with borrowed funds.

However, these changes will probably trigger an adjustment process in the informal credit sector. Thus, it can be assumed that informal providers will withdraw from less profitable segments of the market and focus their resources on borrowers who are perceived as being more creditworthy in an attempt to reduce costs. In addition, informal lenders will have to accept a decline in their income. And because moneylenders' income is an important cost component in the informal sector, this will also lower the costs of informal credit.

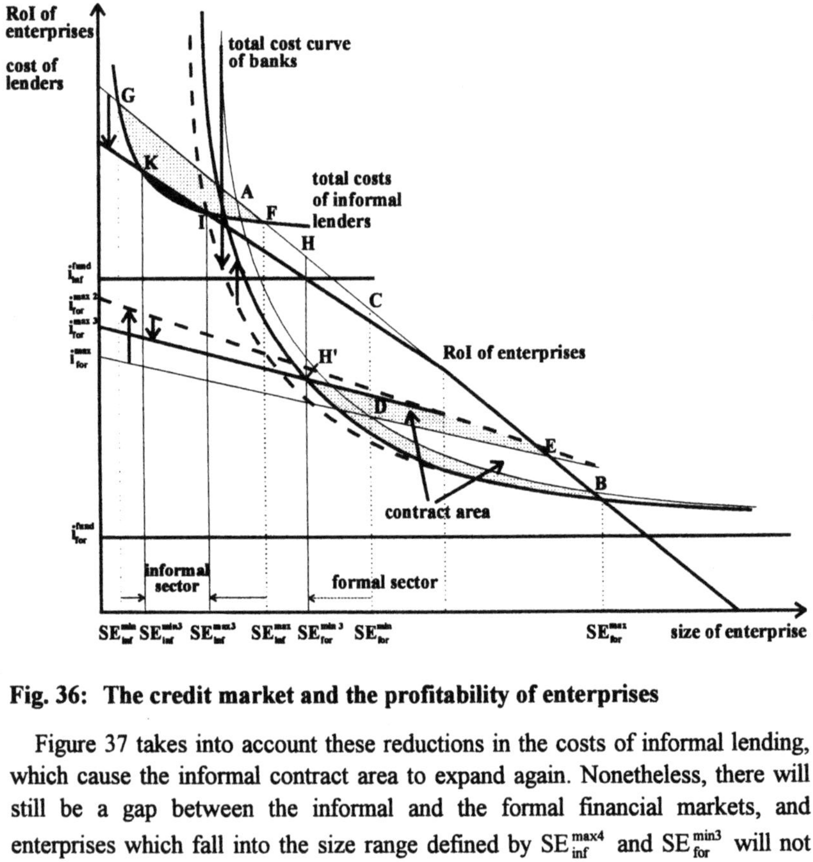

Fig. 36: The credit market and the profitability of enterprises

Figure 37 takes into account these reductions in the costs of informal lending, which cause the informal contract area to expand again. Nonetheless, there will still be a gap between the informal and the formal financial markets, and enterprises which fall into the size range defined by SE_{inf}^{max4} and SE_{for}^{min3} will not have access to credit. However, the RoI decreased in the first place precisely because certain enterprises grew into this particular size range; thus, the growth of larger small enterprises is responsible for the renewed emergence of a gap in the credit market which in turn excludes precisely these businesses from access to credit. In such a situation, the fact that these businesses have expanded places them at a competitive disadvantage, and they will most likely either have to close altogether (because they do not have continued access to loans) or contract until they have returned to their previous size. And bearing in mind that the expansion was facilitated by efficiency gains in lending to small enterprises that were achieved by an effective downscaling programme as described above, this outcome also means that the "success" of the programme will turn out to have been very short-lived, i.e. it will not have made any lasting contribution to alleviating the problem of credit market segmentation.

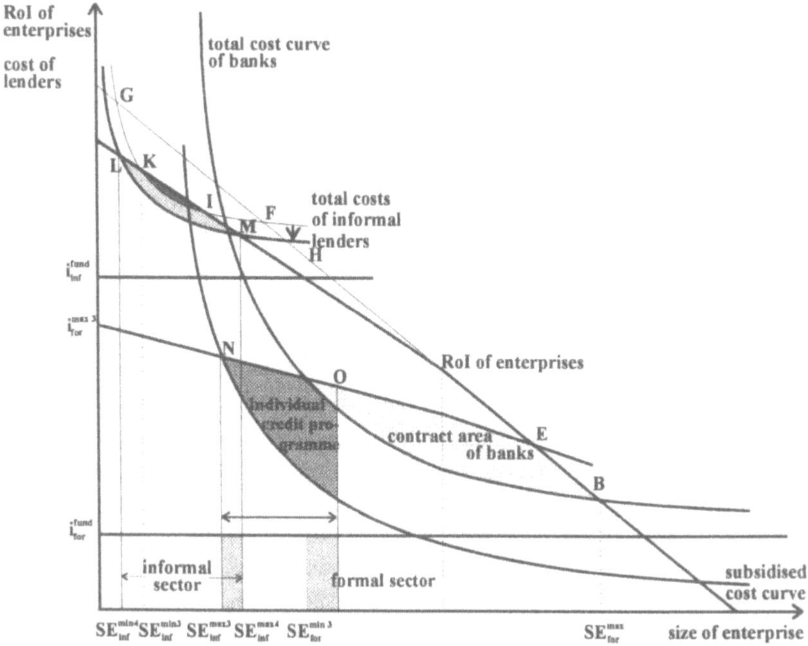

Fig. 37: The need for target group-oriented financial institutions

However, as was demonstrated in the previous section, this type of gap in the financial market can be closed through the establishment of a new, target group-oriented financial institution. Because it is expensive to set up an institution, and because the institution involved here is intended to operate in a relatively unattractive market segment, subsidies will have to be provided, at the very least during a fairly long start-up phase. The "subsidised cost curve" shows the level of risk-related and administrative costs per loan; here, it is assumed that the new institution's funding costs are covered entirely by subsidies. Over time, enhanced efficiency and product innovations should make it possible to reduce the level of subsidisation without causing the curve to shift substantially in the relevant areas.

The segment of the market served by such an institution is shown in the diagram. Small loans can be granted on a cost-covering basis within an area extending as far as point N. As the loan amount increases, profits also rise. Of course, if the institution gradually shifted its focus, moving into the more profitable business of granting large loans, it would also have competitive advantages vis-à-vis the banks due to the subsidies. To prevent this from happening and to ensure that it continues to fulfil its intended objectives, the institution's statutes should stipulate that it shall remain committed to serving its target group as originally defined. This would entail definition of a maximum permissible loan amount, marked by point "O", which might shift over time. Creation of this ceiling would limit the new institution's ability to undercut the banks in their traditional markets. The market segment served by the institution overlaps with both the informal financial market and the formal segment in which the banks operate. As a result, enterprises of various sizes can choose between different financing options, which increases competition. However, it also prevents relatively small changes in individual parameters – such as the reduction in RoI described above – from creating new gaps in the credit market. Only an approach which avoids the emergence of credit gaps can guarantee that a sustainable, long-term development process is initiated in the financial market.

We will now examine the impact which group credit programmes have on the credit market. As was discussed above, such programmes can transfer part of their costs to their customers by making use of peer monitoring and peer pressure to help ensure compliance with repayment obligations, and they grant relatively small loans at "socially acceptable" interest rates. Figure 38 shows in general terms how this approach affects the various relevant parameters; here, group credit programmes charge all customers a uniform interest rate of i^{grup}, and their costs (PQ) are lower than those of individual credit programmes. The money they lose on small loans (SRP) is offset by profits on "larger" loans (RQT). Their customers' incomes rise because they are no longer forced to rely on informal loans, which carry significantly higher interest rates.

For the sake of simplicity, the segment served by group credit programmes and that served by the informal credit sector are exactly congruent in the diagram. In the real world, these two segments will of course not coincide precisely, although they will probably not differ to any significant extent. However, it is easy to see that group credit programmes are not capable of closing the gap in the credit market because their maximum loan amounts are too low. Thus, they do not help to eliminate the structural deficiencies of financial markets.

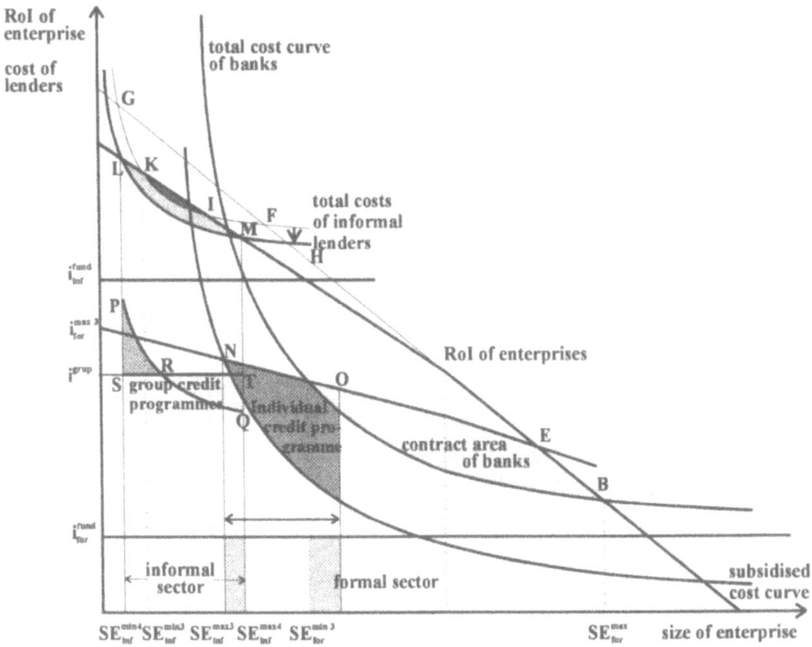

Fig. 38: The impacts of group credit programmes on the financial market

Nonetheless, group credit programmes will always have an impact on the financial market if, as is the case in our example, they are supplemented by individual loan programmes. The individual credit programmes serve to close the credit gap while the group programmes – which are able to grant smaller loans at low interest rates – reduce the interest rate differentials between small and very small loans. They can therefore be regarded as a useful complement to individual credit programmes.

If the measures described thus far have the anticipated effects, the overall demand for credit will increase, which may in turn have adverse indirect impacts. But whether these adverse impacts materialise will depend on the extent to which the local financial market is integrated into the international capital market. If there is a high degree of integration, the domestic interest rate level will be a function of international interest rates and of the specific country risk. A deepening of the capital market will certainly not increase the country risk, and might even lower it. Consequently, the greater demand for credit will also not cause the banks' funding costs to rise, as the additional demand for capital will be met entirely by capital imports.

However, allowance must be made for adverse indirect effects if the country is not fully integrated into the international capital markets, and if, as a consequence, domestic interest rates do not move in tandem with rates on the international capital markets. In this case, greater demand for credit will lead to an increase in domestic interest rates, thus raising the banks' funding costs. The effects of these higher costs are depicted in Figure 39. For the sake of clarity, the parameters for group credit programmes have not been included in this diagram.

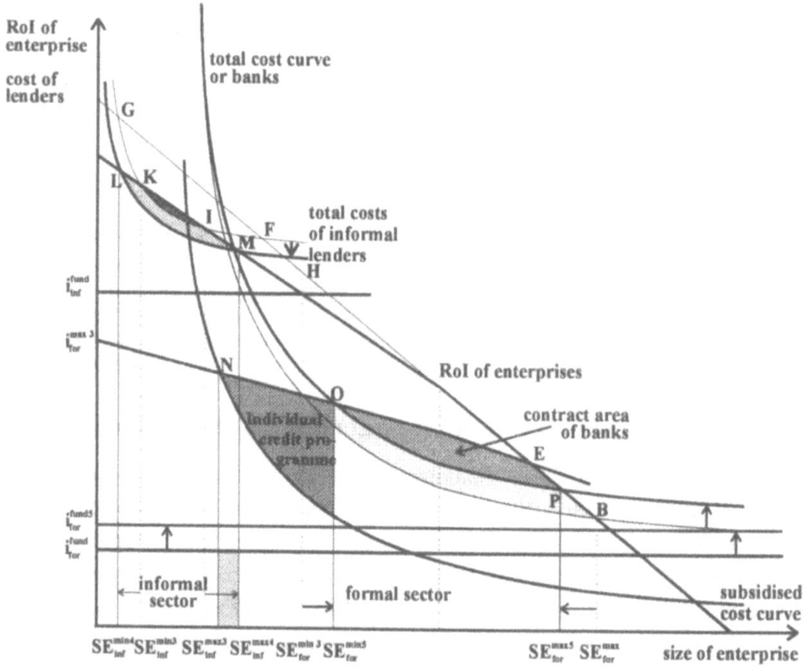

Fig. 39: Impacts of higher capital market interest rates on the credit market

Because informal credit providers do not obtain onlending funds in the formal capital market, and because, in line with the assumptions outlined above, the funding costs of the new, target group-oriented financial institution will be subsidised, an increase in interest rates will only affect bank loans. The total cost function of the banks will shift upward, irrespective of the size of the borrowing enterprise, reducing the contract area to the area shaded in dark grey (OPE) and leading to a corresponding increase in the minimum size (from SE_{for}^{min3} to SE_{for}^{min5})

which qualifies enterprises for loans. In the example shown here, there would be no overlap between the credit supply furnished by the banks and that provided by the newly established institution, but by the same token a gap would be avoided, albeit just barely. Thus, under the set of conditions depicted in the diagram, the scope of the lending activities of the new institution should be expanded to include somewhat larger loans so that a possible upward shift in the minimum enterprise size required for access to bank loans would under no circumstances lead to the emergence of a new gap in the credit market.

2. Impacts on the labour market and the sectoral distribution of enterprises

The impact of small-scale lending is a matter of debate in development policy circles. The concern is often voiced that increasing the availability of small loans merely causes the (unproductive) trade sector to expand. Underlying this concern is the tacit assumption that an improvement in the income of the poor who work in the trade sector would not enhance the welfare of the society as a whole. Without exploring whether such a position is even tenable, this chapter will demonstrate that the point is irrelevant in any case because efficient small-scale lending in fact leads to a disproportionate expansion of the informal production sector.

If we are to investigate the effects of small loan programmes on the sectoral distribution of enterprises, we must first formulate various assumptions regarding the development of factor and goods prices. The following analysis is limited to two cases, the first of which assumes that product markets *and* the markets for capital have been liberalised extensively, i.e. that the economy is open. The funding rates in the formal financial sector in a given country are then determined by international interest rates in conjunction with the country risk, and thus they will not change if the demand for credit on the part of the informal sector increases, as this demand will be completely satisfied by additional capital imports. The prices of tradable goods also remain constant. The second case assumes a closed economy in which an increase in the supply of capital available to the informal sector leads to an outflow of capital from the formal sector, and in which goods prices respond to fluctuations in supply.

a) Small loans in open economies

The impact analysis undertaken in this section is based on the assumption that lending on a greater scale to informal enterprises does not affect the formal sector. Given extensive liberalisation measures, the credit expansion – even if it is the result of more extensive lending activities on the part of banks or of the activities of newly established micro lending institutions that obtain their funds in the banking sector – can be financed with additional capital imports. The additional output generated in the informal industrial sector can either be sold abroad or be used to substitute certain formal-sector products on domestic markets, while the formal-sector goods thus "displaced" by informal products can easily be sold abroad.

Assuming that the increased availability of small-scale loans does not affect the formal sector, we will now examine the ways in which the expanded availability of capital impacts the development of informal industrial sector 2 and the non-tradable goods sector. The analysis will begin by discussing several theoretical aspects, which will then be illustrated with diagrams on the basis of the concepts elaborated in Part II.

The direct effect of an increase in the supply of capital to the informal sector in the form of small loans is that the interest rates paid by informal enterprises will decline. The changes in credit demand in the two segments of the informal sector will be a function of interest rate elasticity. In comparison with trade enterprises, production enterprises operate at a higher level of capital intensity; in addition, their rate of capital turnover is far lower than that of trade enterprises. These two characteristics make their costs much more sensitive to changes in interest rates than those of trade enterprises. Thus, an increase of one percent in the interest rate, for example, will raise the costs of a production operation far more than those of a trade enterprise. In other words, the output, and hence the credit demand, of production enterprises is more interest-elastic than that of trade enterprises. If interest rates are high, there will be only a few industrial enterprises, and they will in turn have a relatively low output. By contrast, lower interest rates will, over the **long term**, result in a disproportionate expansion of output on the part of industrial enterprises.

Over the **short term**, the significant decrease in the cost of capital will initially cause the profits of production enterprises to rise dramatically. In planning for the **medium term**, these enterprises will strive to boost their output, which is a realistic goal for them because their increased profits will enable them, on the one hand, to increase their equity capital, and, on the other, to finance additional projects (at least in part) with relatively inexpensive external capital. Thus, existing businesses will grow substantially. Moreover, entrepreneurs in the trade sector will attempt to move into the production sector, which will have become a more attractive market than trade, provided that the additional know-how required to do so is not so substantial as to act as a market entry barrier. In other words, the number of production enterprises will increase.

Changes in product prices are a function of both the nature and size of the markets on which enterprises can sell their products and the elasticity of demand. The output of the production sector is tradable, and depending on their quality, the products involved can also be sold on international markets. The larger the potential sales market, the less pronounced the change in price will be. Indeed, the prices of goods which can be sold on international markets should not be affected at all. It was assumed above that far-reaching liberalisation measures have substantially reduced trade barriers; as a result of these liberalisation measures, industrial good 2 can be sold abroad, and its price will be determined exogenously in the world market. The option of selling industrial good 2 in other countries keeps the prices of informally produced goods from falling even if they are not of sufficient quality to be traded on the world market, provided they can substitute formal industrial good 2 in the domestic market.

Assuming that price effects remain very limited, the increased availability of capital will cause labour productivity – and thus, over the long term, the wage rate – to rise. It is impossible to arrive at conclusions regarding the changes in the non-tradable goods sector for two reasons: labour migrates to the production sector, but at the same time the substantial capital expansion in the production sector does not automatically rule out an increase in the supply of capital available to the trade sector. In other words, there may be an increase in the availability of capital in both sectors. As capital was previously quite scarce in the trade sector, even a small increase in the capital supply is more than enough to compensate for the migration of labour from trade to production.

This line of reasoning will now be illustrated with the help of several diagrams. The first diagram, Figure 40, shows how informal enterprises are affected over the short term when cheaper financing options are available to them. If we depict these effects on the basis of the Heckscher-Ohlin model as presented in Chapter II.2, the factor price line for the informal sector rotates upward; i.e. the costs of producing one unit of output (US$ 1) decrease, enabling the enterprise to earn additional profits. It is clear that the profits of production enterprises will increase to a greater extent than those of trade enterprises (areas shaded in grey).

The opportunity to earn higher profits will induce enterprises to expand their output. However, an increase in production requires, among other things, additional workers, who must be recruited from other enterprises.[63] As enterprises compete for labour, wage rates in the informal sector will increase until output has expanded to the point where further growth will not result in additional profits.

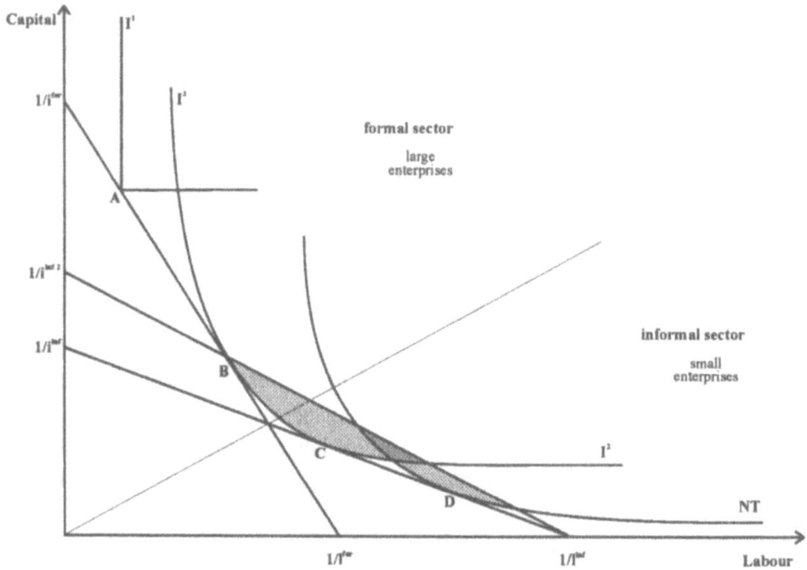

Fig. 40: The short-term effects of lower interest rates

Figure 41 depicts the new state of equilibrium. If we assume that the goods produced by industrial sector 2 can be traded on international markets, and that, as a result, an increase in output will not cause the price of these products to decrease, informal wage rates will rise to a level of l^{for2}, i.e. the factor price line rotates downward until it is just barely touching the isoquant for industrial sector 2. Because there is no longer a point of intersection or tangency between the factor price line and the NT isoquant, enterprises in the non-tradable goods sector will invariably incur losses if prices remain constant. However, we have already demonstrated that a number of entrepreneurs in this sector would migrate to industrial sector 2, where they can earn greater profits. Thus, the supply of non-tradable goods will continue to contract (at least in relative terms)

63 This statement is based on the assumption that the informal sector employs all workers who are unable to find employment in the informal sector; i.e. that there is no reservoir of unemployed workers.

until the prices in this sector have increased sufficiently to cause the isoquant to shift (downwards and to the left) toward the origin until it reaches the position designated by NT'. Therefore, in the new state of equilibrium, the wage level in the informal sector will increase, as will the prices of non-tradable goods and services.

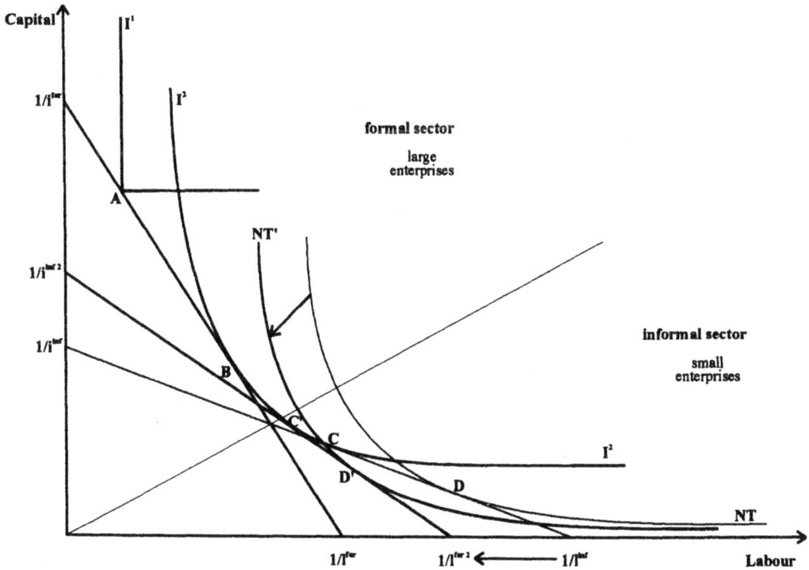

Fig. 41: Changes in factor and product prices given lower interest rates

How do the inflow of capital and lower interest rates alter the sectoral distribution of economic activity in the informal sector? As was demonstrated above, changes in the sectoral distribution of enterprises are a function of interest rate elasticities. For this reason, the more interest rates decrease, the greater the extent to which the sectoral distribution will change. In order to gauge more precisely the various possible effects of lower rates, we shall first assess the impact of a moderate drop in interest rates on the basis of the RYBCZYNSKI theorem,[64] following which the impact of a more substantial decrease is illustrated with the help of the STOLPER-SAMUELSON concept.

Figure 42 shows the distribution of factors between the two segments of the informal sector, both before and after the supply of capital has expanded. Before the supply of capital increases, and before interest rates drop, non-tradable

---

64 For more information on the foundations of the RYBCZYNSKI theorem, cf. RYBCZYNSKI, 1955.

goods are produced with combinations of factors that correspond to the dotted line 0D; industrial goods 2 are produced with factor combinations that correspond to line 0C. FS^1 represents the total stock of factors available to the informal sector; informal industrial sector 2 uses the factors represented by line 0F, while non-tradable goods are produced using the factors represented by 0E.

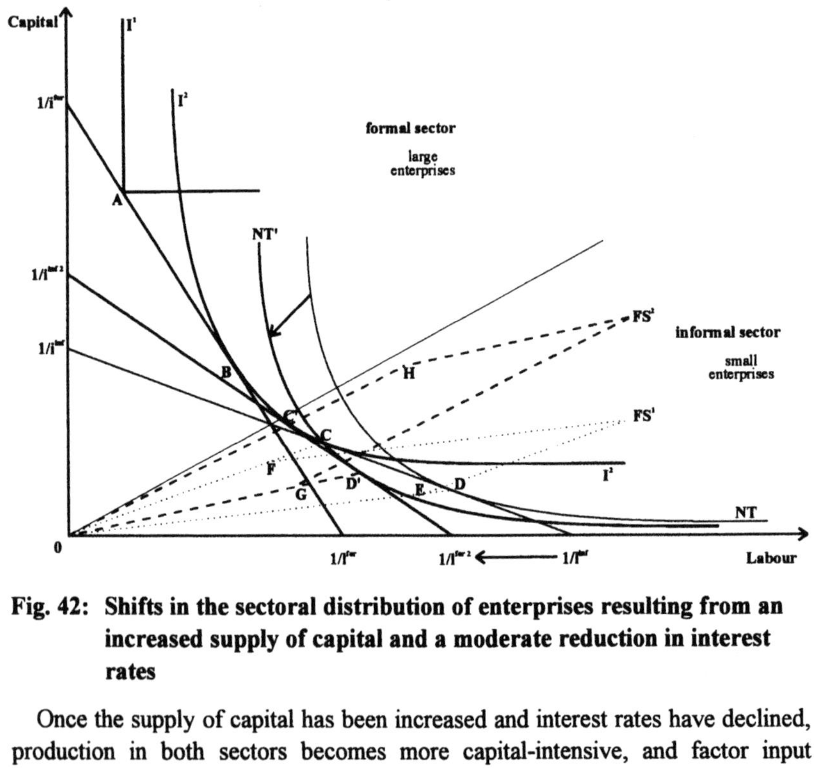

Fig. 42: Shifts in the sectoral distribution of enterprises resulting from an increased supply of capital and a moderate reduction in interest rates

Once the supply of capital has been increased and interest rates have declined, production in both sectors becomes more capital-intensive, and factor input intensities correspond to the slopes of the broken lines 0D' and 0C'. The inflow of capital has increased the factor supply to FS^2. If factors are distributed efficiently, then industrial sector 2 will now have access to a quantity of factors represented by 0H; in other words, the quantity of both labour and capital available to this sector will increase substantially. At the same time, the volume of factors available for the production of non-tradable goods drops to 0G – i.e. output in this sector decreases.

If interest rates drop more sharply, though, the sectoral effects may be different. In Figure 43, the supply of capital has increased by the same amount as in the previous example (i.e. it has doubled); however, it is assumed that the factor price ratio has changed more dramatically. This assumption is reflected in the steeper incline of the factor price line. In this example, there is not only a disproportionate increase in output in industrial sector 2, with factor utilisation rising from CB to CD, but also a rise in the volume of non-tradable goods produced, as is reflected in the shift of isoquant NH to NH^2.

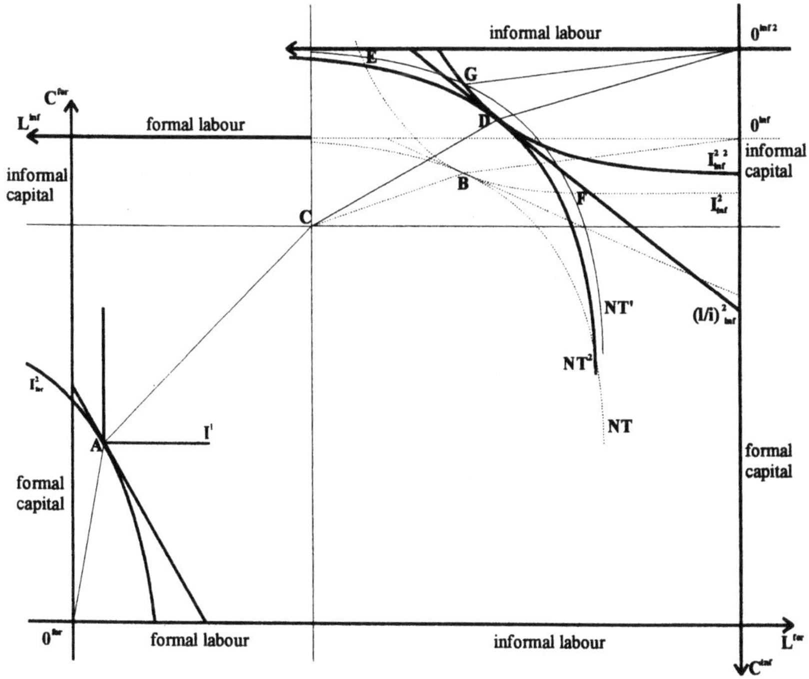

Fig. 43: Shifts in the sectoral distribution of enterprises resulting from capital inflows and a more substantial decrease in interest rates

In this example, a substantial decrease in interest rates does more to reduce the degree of segmentation in the economy as a whole than a moderate drop in rates. At the same time, however, activity in the non-tradable goods sector – activity which many consider to be unproductive – also increases, although proportionally the increase is smaller than that which takes place in industrial sector 2. This indicates that here, the demand for non-tradable goods has a higher income elasticity than it did in the previous example. Because the factor price line has a steeper slope, the price of non-tradable goods must have increased more than in our previous example, and thus a simultaneous expansion in the output of non-tradable goods can occur only if the income elasticity of the demand for these goods is relatively high. Because production in this sector is labour-intensive, this expansion is only feasible if both the industrial and the non-tradable goods sector begin to operate at an even higher level of capital intensity. As a result, if the capital supply has expanded, growth in the industrial sector, where production is more capital-intensive than in the non-tradable goods sector, will not be as pronounced as it was in the preceding example.

We must now ask whether an inflow of foreign capital and a concomitant drop in interest rates might under certain circumstances cause the output of tradable goods to decrease. In the following, we will demonstrate that such an outcome is possible, but only if small-scale credit programmes are implemented in such a way that supply and demand are no longer balanced by market forces.

The inflow of foreign capital is usually associated with the establishment of a small-scale lending institution which not only "channels" this capital, but also uses more efficient credit technologies and is typically subsidised; in other words, it does not aim to maximise its profits, but rather sets its prices (interest rates) at a "socially responsible" level. Because this institution earns only a small profit, or perhaps even incurs losses, only the funds provided by the donor or donors – a small amount in relative terms – will be available to the informal sector as additional capital. At the same time, though, interest rates on loans to enterprises granted by this institution decrease considerably.

This situation is depicted in Figure 44. As in the previous example, interest rates on informal loans fall to $i^{inf\,2}$, while the supply of capital available to the informal sector expands only slightly, increasing to FS^3.

This set of circumstances apparently causes the factor input in the non-tradable sector to increase sharply (from 0E to 0G'), while the factor input in the informal industrial sector contracts significantly (from 0F to 0H'). However, such an outcome is counterintuitive, for we have already demonstrated that the incentive to expand output created by a decrease in interest rates will be far more pronounced in the industrial sector than in the non-tradable sector. It is also worthy of note that in the state of equilibrium derived here, the production of non-tradable goods increases considerably, yet at the same time prices in this sector (must) increase, as is illustrated by the compression of the isoquant (downwards and to the left) toward the origin.

How can we explain these paradoxical outcomes? The model used here assumes that perfect competition exists – i.e. that factor prices must reflect the relative scarcity of factors. However, the supply of capital has increased only slightly, while interest rates have fallen significantly (at least in relative terms). As was mentioned above, though, the new, lower interest rate level was not created by the unconstrained operation of the forces in a free market; rather, the new rates represent "socially responsible" prices which have been set at levels lower than those in effect on the open market. As a consequence, newly established lending institutions of the type involved here will be unable to satisfy more than a small portion of the demand for their loans, i.e. they will be forced to ration credit.

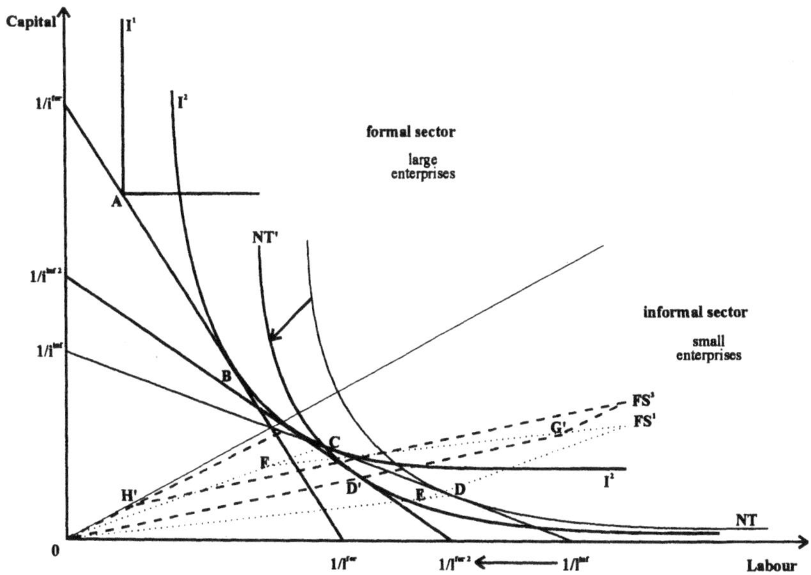

Fig. 44: Possible changes in sectoral distribution as a product of a reduction in interest rates and only a slight increase in the supply of capital?

The vast majority of micro entrepreneurs will therefore have to continue to base their production cost calculations on the "old" factor costs. As a result, neither interest rates nor the wage level will change in the informal sector as a whole, and thus the sectoral distribution of production will also remain unchanged. Those enterprises that are able to obtain inexpensive loans from the new institution will not need to increase their employees' wages; however, access to the cheap funds will enable them to lower their capital costs and increase their profits as shown in our analysis as presented in Figure 40. In other words, it is important to bear in mind the consequences of setting interest rates at "socially responsible" levels. Small loan programmes that give priority to keeping their interest rates low rather than earning high profits – which would enable them to expand the scope of their capital intermediation – enable their customers to achieve a disproportionately large increase in their incomes. But because they are not able to engage in intermediation on a significant scale, they are also not capable of initiating lasting structural changes that would raise the overall level of efficiency and labour productivity in the informal sector over the long term.

For this reason, small-scale lending institutions should set their interest rates high enough to ensure a favourable earnings position. This in turn will enable them to obtain additional external capital, e.g. from banks, which they can use to steadily expand the supply of capital available to the informal sector. Use of such an approach will also ensure that there will be a disproportionately large increase in the output of tradable goods, and that informal wage levels will rise.

b) Small loans in closed economies

This section examines the effects of small-loan programmes in countries in which no extensive liberalisation measures have been carried out (closed economies). In such economies, one cannot expect that there will be an inflow of foreign capital, or that goods prices will remain constant. The total supply of capital in the economy thus remains constant, which is why an increase in the capital supply available to the informal sector must inevitably lead to a corresponding outflow of capital from the formal sector.

We will also formulate assumptions concerning the development of output and prices in the individual sectors, which in principle is a function of the respective elasticities of supply and demand. Thus, many different scenarios are conceivable. For the sake of simplicity, in the following only *one* possible scenario is presented, in which output and prices remain constant both in industrial sector 1 and in the sector for non-tradable goods and services. This is a fairly good approximation of how output and prices are in fact likely to develop, as the demand for what is produced in these sectors varies only slightly. On the one hand, the improvements in efficiency described below lead to an increase in real incomes; on the other hand, the price of industrial good 2 can be expected to fall, i.e. the relative prices of the other products will increase. In the following, it is assumed that the changes in incomes and relative prices will be such that these two effects will just barely balance each other out with respect to the demand for industrial good 1 and non-tradables.

In the following analysis, we will first investigate the ways in which an increase in the supply of credit available to the informal sector impacts factor prices and factor input intensities using the HECKSCHER-OHLIN model. The sectoral impacts will then be described with the help of the STOLPER-SAMUELSON theorem.

As was shown in the preceding section, an expansion in the credit supply to the informal sector causes the interest rates paid by enterprises in this sector to drop (from i^{inf} to $i^{inf\,2}$). Lower interest rates will benefit in particular the enterprises in informal industrial sector 2, enabling them to increase their output and demand credit in ever larger quantities. Because the funds used to meet this expanding demand are diverted from the formal sector, the supply of capital available to the formal sector decreases; consequently, formal interest rates rise from i^{for} to $i^{for\,2}$. These short-term effects are depicted in Figure 45 by the broken lines.

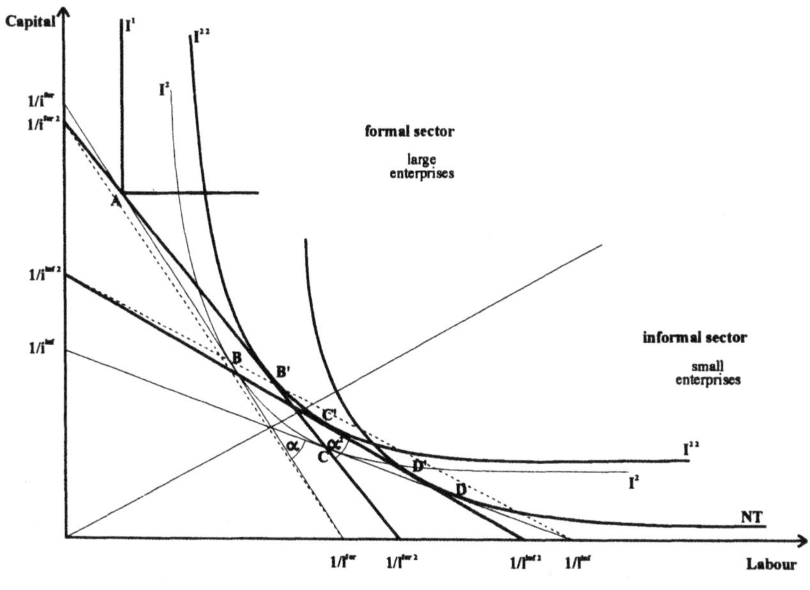

Fig. 45: The impact of small-scale lending in a closed economy

In this situation, formal enterprises will incur losses, as their costs will exceed their revenues. Enterprises in industrial sector 1 are affected to a greater extent than businesses in industrial sector 2. Informal enterprises will achieve extraordinary profits, in particular those in industrial sector 2, which are able to continuously expand their production. The resulting drop in prices, which is represented by the shift in isoquant I^2 to $I^{2\,2}$, further diminishes the earnings of the formal enterprises in this sector.

The existence of extraordinary profits or losses suggests that what we are looking at is a transition phase rather than a state of equilibrium. Because the earnings situation of formal enterprises has deteriorated, formal-sector wages drop from w^{for} to w^{for2}. At the same time, informal enterprises now have a favourable earnings situation and, because their operations are more capital-intensive, their labour productivity also increases. These two factors cause the informal wage level to rise from w^{inf} to w^{inf2}, which in turn reduces the extent of factor market segmentation, as is revealed by the smaller differential between the slopes of the factor price lines (α and α^2). Income is distributed more evenly throughout the economy (see Chapter II.4).

In the new state of equilibrium, prices in industrial sector 1 and in the sector for non-tradable goods and services remain constant. However, activity in the sector for non-tradable goods and services is now more capital-intensive, i.e. labour is replaced with capital (shift from D to D'). The level of capital intensity falls in the formal part of industrial sector 2 (from B to B') at the same time as it increases in the informal production enterprises (from C to C').

The effects on the sectoral distribution of enterprises will now be illustrated using the STOLPER-SAMUELSON theorem (see Figure 46). Small-scale lending to informal enterprises increases the supply of capital in the informal sector; thus, the factor box which represents the factor supply available to the informal sector expands from 0^{inf} C to 0^{inf} C'. Correspondingly, the factor box representing the formal sector's factor supply contracts from 0^{for}C to 0^{for}C'. Thus, it is implicitly assumed that the formal sector does not need to discharge any of its workers, i.e. that the decrease in the supply of capital is compensated for by what is now a more labour-intensive mode of production in formal industrial sector 2, without employment being impacted.

In keeping with the assumptions outlined above, output in I^1 remains constant, and thus, as a result of the linear-limitational production function, factor utilisation does not change. At the same time, because less capital is available, production operations in formal industrial sector 2 are less capital-intensive (AC' has a more gentle slope than AC), and output decreases.

However, this drop in output is more than offset by the enterprises operating in the informal part of the sector. This becomes apparent if one initially assumes that all of the capital diverted from the formal sector were to flow into the informal production sector, enabling informal production enterprises to utilise the factors represented by segment C'B. In this case, the factor supply available to industrial sector 2 as a whole does not change. The internal redistribution of capital from formal enterprises with a capital-intensive mode of production to informal enterprises with a labour-intensive mode of production reduces the first-degree efficiency losses derived in Part II and thus increases overall output.

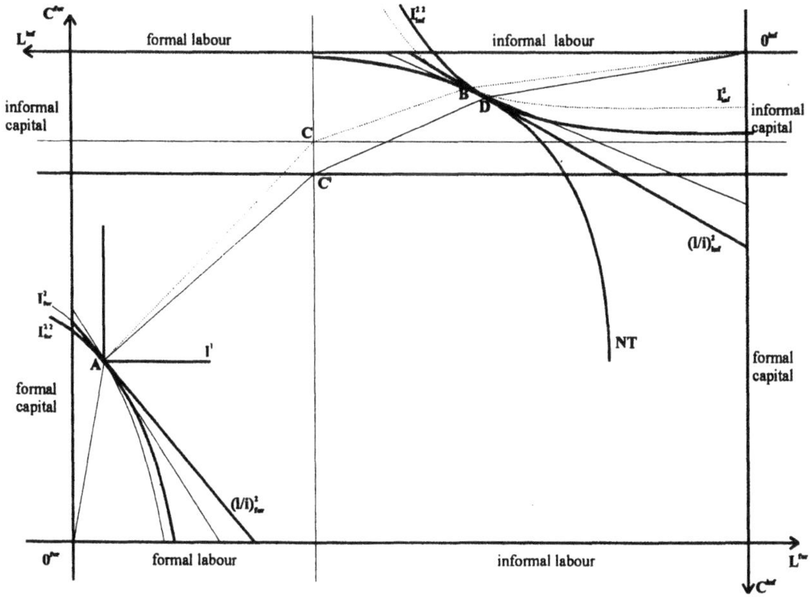

Fig. 46: The sectoral effects of small loan programmes in a closed economy

Moreover, a substitution of factors takes place between the two segments of the informal sector, because, in the situation described above, the isoquants of these two segments intersect. Consequently, the factor markets operating in the informal sector now once again effect a reallocation of factors. If the output of the sector producing non-tradable goods remains constant, this sector can utilise the factors defined by 0^{inf} D instead of 0^{inf} B. In other words, it can produce at a higher level of capital intensity. Consequently, the factors available to informal industrial sector 2 are now represented by C'D instead of C'B, which means that the output of this sector will again increase (slightly), reducing the second-degree efficiency losses.

In general, improving the supply of small-scale loans in a closed economy will reduce the efficiency losses derived in Part II; as a result, industrial output can be increased. However, the sectoral effects cannot be defined both precisely *and* in general terms because, unlike the situation in an open economy, changes in the prices of tradable goods must also be expected.

However, we can in effect rule out the possibility that only the output of non-tradable goods and services will rise. Indeed, if the increase in output were restricted exclusively to the non-tradables sector, the relative increase in wage costs would necessarily cause the prices of this sector's products to rise as well, despite the considerable expansion in the volume of production. Yet such price increases would only be feasible if demand for non-tradable goods and services were highly income-elastic; typically, however, the income elasticity of demand for such goods and services tends to be quite low, or even negative. Thus, improving the credit supply for informal enterprises will lead to an increase in the output of tradable goods in both open and closed economies.

3. Income-related effects

This chapter examines the income-related effects of small loan programmes. Unfortunately, conventional impact analyses are limited to an investigation of the ways in which small-scale lending programmes *directly* affect borrowers' incomes. These direct effects comprise, on the one hand, the interest rate differential between the programmes' loans and alternative sources of financing, and, on the other, the additional profits that entrepreneurs are able to make because they have been able to expand their businesses by using the borrowed funds. The effects captured by this traditional approach are depicted in Figure 47. Access to inexpensive loans causes the cost or supply function of an enterprise to shift downward from S_1 to S_2, so that the profit per unit produced and the supply increase simultaneously. The increase in the producer's surplus accruing to the owner of the enterprise is represented by the area shaded in grey.

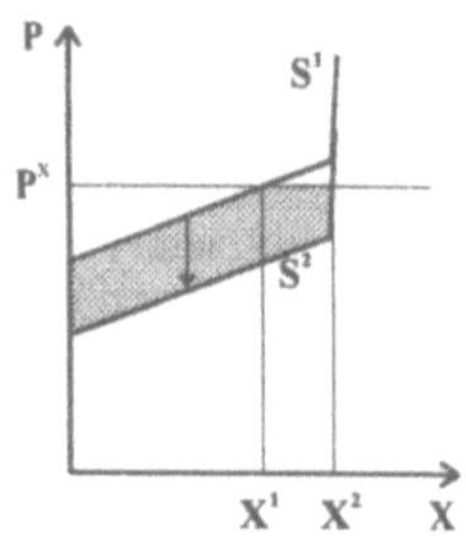

Fig. 47: The direct income-related effects of small loans

The extent to which a small loan programme contributes to combating poverty (measured in US$) is then determined by multiplying the average increase in the borrowers' income (in US$) by the number of borrowers and the percentage of borrowers who are poor. If, for example, a small loan programme causes the income of its customers to increase by US$ 10 per month on average, and 60% of a total of 10,000 borrowers are poor, the programme's contribution to the alleviation of poverty would be US$ 10 * 10,000 * 60% = US$ 60,000/month.[65] However, this will only prove to be an accurate method of gauging the income-related effects of such a programme if its outreach is quite limited, i.e. if the group of borrowers it serves does not represent a significant share of the overall group of small entrepreneurs. Otherwise, the effects on the market induced by the cost reductions which are made possible by the availability of inexpensive loans must also be taken into consideration; likewise, one must also take into account the effects on the incomes of other suppliers of goods and services who did not receive credit, as well as the effects on the incomes of consumers. The following section contains an impact analysis which captures these indirect effects. Subsequently, the theoretical implications of the analysis are examined and verified in the light of selected findings of an empirical study which, however, looks only at the direct effects of small loan programmes on borrowers' incomes as measured by the amount of increase over their previous income levels.

a) Impact on the income of customers, non-customers and consumers

In analysing the income-related effects of small loan programmes for all market participants, we shall in the following differentiate between loans to borrowers who intend to start a new business, and loans to existing enterprises. For each of these two groups, the situation prior to the introduction of small-scale lending is described, first assuming a low level of market penetration, and then assuming a higher degree of market penetration.

Loans to entrepreneurs who wish to establish a new business

The loans provided by group credit programmes are intended to offer the poorest of the poor an alternative to unemployment or underemployment and enable them to earn their living as self-employed persons. They use the funds to establish new enterprises, which in turn have exclusive access to the inexpensive loans offered by the group programmes.

Prior to the introduction of loan programmes which cater to new enterprises, existing businesses are the sole suppliers in the market. Let us assume that the supply function of existing enterprises is represented by the line S^E in Figure 48. This function can then be applied to the market as a whole, where, given a

65 Cf. HULME/MOSLEY, 1996, p. 182-5.

demand function of D^{total}, price P^1 emerges. The producer's surplus is represented by the dark-grey area; the consumer surplus corresponds to the area shaded in light grey.

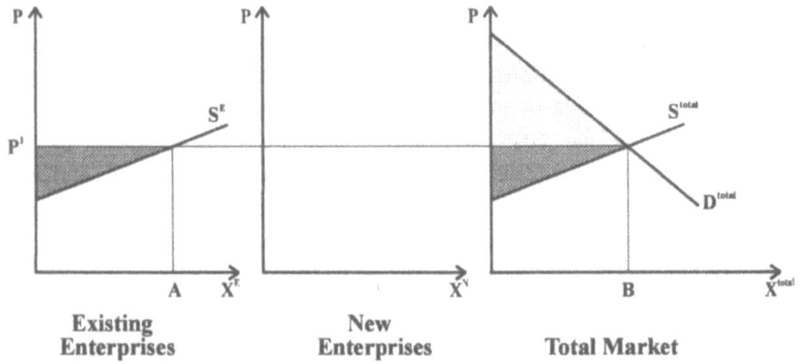

Fig. 48: The situation prior to the issue of loans to new enterprises

Small loans are then granted to a group of borrowers who intend to establish new enterprises; initially, the group of loan recipients will be relatively small. These borrowers have little experience, which tends to increase their costs; at the same time, however, they have access to inexpensive loans, which tends to reduce their costs. In the following, it is assumed that, although the cost function of new businesses initially exceeds that of existing enterprises, the additional costs they incur when expanding their output are lower than those incurred by existing businesses because they can finance such expansions with inexpensive loans. The supply function of new enterprises (S^{N2} in Figure 49) is thus more price-elastic than that of existing businesses. However, new businesses cannot expand their output indefinitely because once they reach a certain size, they simply do not have sufficient "management capacity" to grow any further. At the point on the diagram that represents this maximum enterprise size, the supply function angles sharply upward (the supply function of existing enterprises "angles upward" in essentially the same way, but not in the market segments relevant for this analysis).

In the market as a whole, the two supply functions are aggregated to form a new total supply function, $S^{total\ 2}$, which causes the price of the product in question to drop to P^2. The area shaded in dark grey represents the increase in the producer's surplus and the consumer surplus, while the decrease in the producer's rent accruing to existing entrepreneurs is represented by the light grey area. It is clear that the income of borrowers being served by the new small-scale loan programmes has in fact increased. In the example shown above, the consumer surplus increases by a far larger amount than the producer's surplus accruing to new entrepreneurs, and thus consumers are the biggest "winners". At the same time, the producer's surplus accruing to existing enterprises decreases considerably. It should be borne in mind that the existing entrepreneurs who must compete with new businesses are usually also poor or exist just above the poverty line.

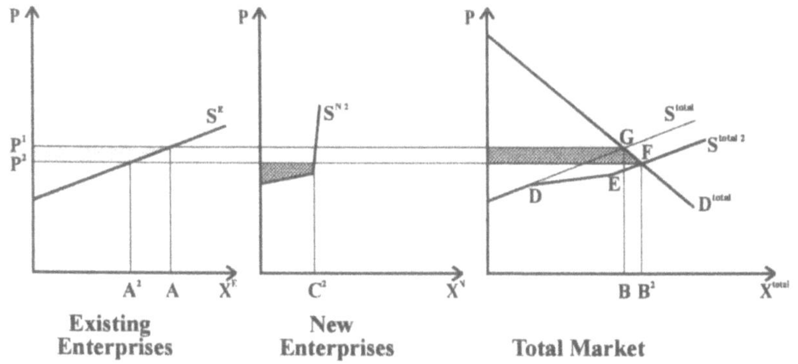

Fig. 49: The effects of moderate lending to new enterprises

The total increase in the producer's and consumer's surplus resulting from the availability of inexpensive loans corresponds to the area DEFG, and is thus smaller than the increase in the consumer surplus. Therefore, the introduction of small-scale lending programmes means that as a group, producers suffer a loss in the amount of the surplus which accrues to them. Thus, in addition to the absolute increase in income, there is also a redistribution of wealth from producers to consumers – a fact that should always be borne in mind if the consumers in a given case do not fall into the category of the "needy poor".

In the most extreme case, goods will be produced exclusively for the purpose of "exporting" them to a relatively distant (and perhaps much wealthier) city, or even to another country. In such a situation, the incomes of the inhabitants of the region that was supposed to benefit from the introduction of small-scale lending will decline overall, despite the fact that the new entrepreneurs who obtain credit from small loan programmes will be able to increase their incomes.

Is this scenario realistic? First of all, an objection must be raised to this last line of reasoning: It is highly unlikely that the region in question would be confronted with such a low elasticity of demand in its "export market". In fact, the demand for exports should prove to be infinitely elastic – after all, the producers of this region are price takers. If this is so, then the existing enterprises should not have to accept any losses in the producer's surplus that accrues to them, while the increases in the surplus accruing to new entrepreneurs would be even greater.

Does this mean that the above objection is irrelevant? By no means. The argument advanced to show that the assumption of a very low elasticity of demand is incorrect would only be valid if no small loan programmes were implemented in the regions where the competitors of the borrowing enterprises operate. But given the strong movement to promote small-scale lending, it is extremely unlikely that such a situation would arise. However, if new businesses in all regions in which competing suppliers operate have access to small loans, the same line of reasoning that was found to apply above will also be valid for the group of suppliers as a whole, i.e. consumers will indeed profit at the expense of producers.

Does this mean that small loan programmes should not be established? Here again, the answer is "no". First of all, even if a given region decided not to participate in small-loan programmes, it would find it difficult or impossible to prevent such programmes from being established in other areas. And as the only region to forgo the benefits of small-scale lending, it would stand to lose the most because no new businesses would be founded in this region. Such a region would contain only "existing enterprises" – i.e. "losers". Secondly, in the two preceding chapters it was demonstrated that efficient small-scale lending can eliminate or reduce structural problems that impede the efficiency of the financial market and help to preserve factor market segmentation. Thirdly, it is certainly possible to avoid the above dilemma by pursuing a strategy of flexible adaptation to market conditions: production must shift to areas in which demand is more elastic, i.e. more profitable niches must be sought and found. Implementing such a strategy is the only way to effectively address the root causes of poverty.

Figure 50 depicts more dramatically the need for supporting strategies in the effort to fight poverty. This diagram shows the effects on income when twice as many new enterprises receive loans as in the previous scenario. The decrease in the producer's surplus accruing to existing enterprises is even greater than it was in the last scenario, while the increase in the producer's surplus accruing to new enterprises has declined significantly. By contrast, the consumer surplus has again risen sharply.

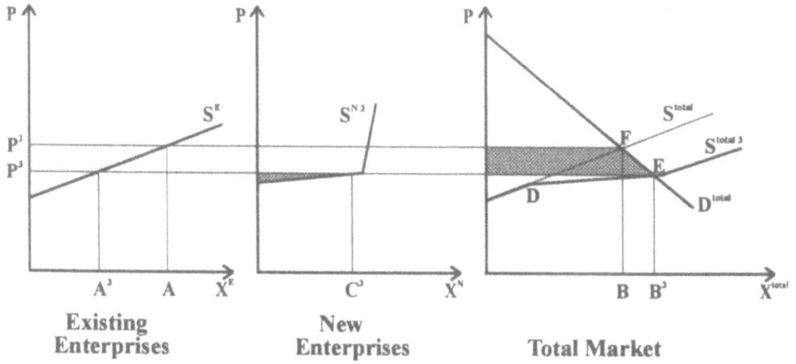

Fig. 50: The effects of more extensive lending to new enterprises

The sum total of all changes in the surpluses accruing to producers and consumers, represented by the area DEF, is now much smaller than the increase in the consumer surplus; in other words, as a group, producers now suffer very high losses in the surplus accruing to them. Moreover, it is clear that the income of new borrowers is now very low and is probably highly susceptible to external shocks (see also Section IV.3.b). Whenever members of the target group of the "needy poor" do not account for the majority of consumers, granting small loans to new entrepreneurs throughout the country or region in question will further exacerbate poverty unless parallel efforts are made to shift the focus of production towards goods which exhibit a higher elasticity of demand.

Are there circumstances under which the producers as a group can also increase the surplus which accrues to them? Over the medium term, this is indeed feasible. Specifically, it can occur when new enterprises have acquired sufficient experience and know-how to operate as efficiently as existing ones. Once they have achieved this level of efficiency, their access to inexpensive loans will enable them to operate at lower cost than existing enterprises, and their supply curve will shift downward (see S^{N4} in Figure 51). In the example shown below, existing enterprises have nearly been forced out of the market, and are only able to produce quantity A^4. Once again, the amount of the losses in the producer's surplus accruing to existing enterprises increases, but the increment in the surplus accruing to new enterprises is much greater, and indeed it is more than sufficient to offset the losses incurred by the existing enterprises. Thus, overall, the producer's surplus will increase.

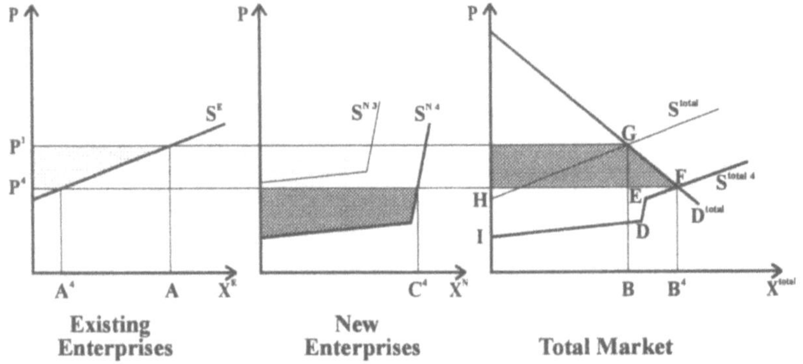

Fig. 51: The medium-term effects of lending to new entrepreneurs

However, the producer's surplus can only increase on this scale so long as new enterprises produce at their capacity limit (above the "angle" shown in the diagram). Any increase in capacity now causes prices to drop sharply, as the market clears in those segments in which demand is highly inelastic. Over the long term, this will cause the producer's surplus accruing to new entrepreneurs to decline again, with the overall effect on the producer's income again becoming negative.

Loans to existing enterprises

The bulk of the loans issued to existing enterprises are provided by individual loan programmes and downscaling projects. In the following, it is assumed that the cost and supply functions of borrowing enterprises are not significantly different from those of enterprises that do not receive credit. Figure 52 shows the situation prior to the receipt of loans; here, a distinction has already been made between future customers and non-customers of small loan programmes, i.e. future borrowers and non-borrowers. It is assumed that one-third of the enterprises will eventually have access to credit. Because there are fewer potential customers than non-customers, the supply function of the future customers is steeper than that of the non-customers, although the elasticity of supply is the same for all enterprises.

The supply functions of the two groups – future non-customers (S^{NC}) and future customers (S^C) – aggregate in the overall market to form total supply function S^{total}, for which, given demand of D^{total}, price P^1 emerges. The producer's surplus, both for the respective groups of entrepreneurs and for the enterprise sector as a whole, corresponds to the area shaded in dark grey. The consumer surplus is represented by the light-grey area.

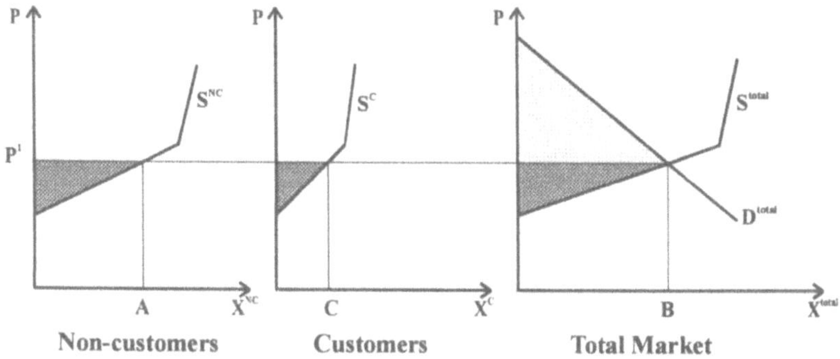

Fig. 52: The situation prior to the introduction of small loans for existing enterprises

Customers now receive loans that are cheaper than those previously available to them in the informal credit market; as a result, their supply function shifts downward (see Figure 53). They will thus expand their output from C to C^2 and operate at their capacity limit. In the market as a whole, this gives rise to a new supply function, $S^{total\ 2}$; consequently, the quantity sold increases to B^2, while the price decreases to P^2.

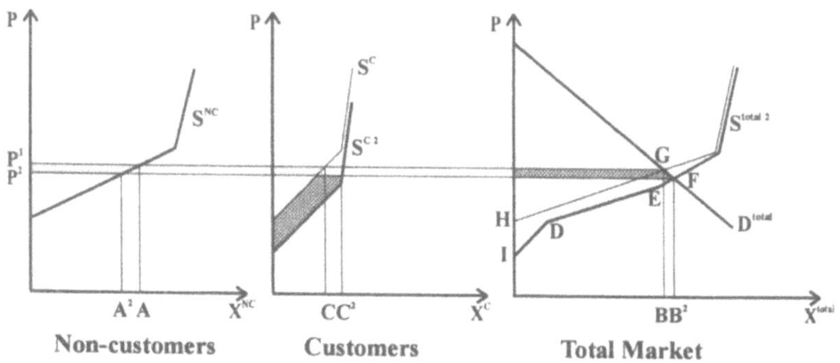

Fig. 53: The effects of lending to a small portion of existing enterprises

The increase in surpluses that is induced by the introduction of small-scale lending corresponds to the dark-grey areas; the decrease in surpluses is represented by the areas shaded in light grey. Thus, on the producers' side, non-customers must accept a decrease in the surplus that accrues to them, while the producer's surplus that accrues to customers increases by an amount that corresponds to the difference between the dark and light-grey areas. The consumer surplus also increases. The total increase in the surpluses accruing to producers and consumers corresponds to the area DEFGHI, and is clearly larger than the increase in the consumer surplus. Thus, the income of the producers as a group increases, although at the same time there is also a redistribution of income within this group from non-customers to the customers of the small-scale lending institutions.

If the scope of lending activities is now extended, an expanding share of producers will have access to inexpensive loans. Figure 54 depicts a situation in which two-thirds of producers receive credit.

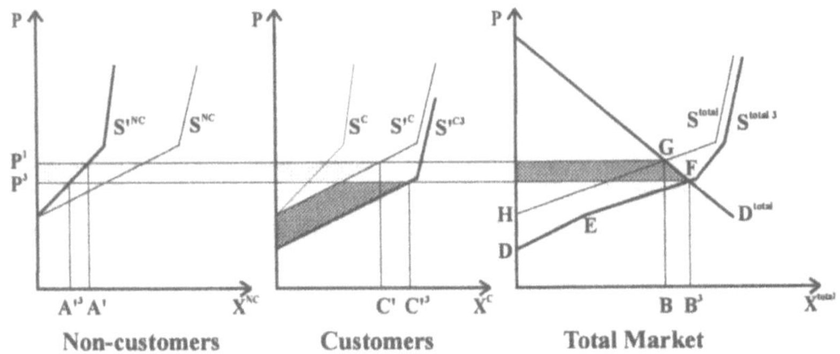

Fig. 54: Effects of lending to the majority of existing enterprises

In analysing the diagram, we must first of all bear in mind that the group of customers is larger. Consequently, the supply function of this group would have been longer and flatter than it was before any enterprises received credit, and would have corresponded to the function S'^{C}. The opposite is true for non-customers, whose supply function, S'^{NC}, would have been shorter and sloped upward more sharply.

In the market as a whole, the supply functions S'^{NC} and S'^{C3} now aggregate to form total supply function $S^{total\ 3}$, causing the supply to increase to B^3 while the price falls to P^3. The increase in the surpluses accruing to producers and consumers, as compared with the situation prior to the introduction of the credit programme, is represented by the area shaded in dark grey, while the decrease in surpluses accruing to producers corresponds to the light-grey area. The overall increase in the surpluses is represented by the area DEFGH, which in turn is larger than the increase in the consumer surplus. Therefore, producers as a group also benefit in this case. At the same time, there is a relatively large redistribution of income from non-customers to customers of the credit programmes (the producer's surplus accruing to non-customers decreases by more than half).

According to this analysis, small-scale lending to existing enterprises has a more favourable impact on the income of producers than lending to new entrepreneurs. To a large extent, however, the difference in the two outcomes is contingent on the assumption that the introduction of lending to existing enterprises will alter the position of the supply function, but not its slope. In general, the smaller the increase in the elasticity of supply induced by small-scale lending and the greater the elasticity of demand in the relevant product markets, the more favourable will be the impact of small-scale lending on the incomes of producers as a group. If the elasticity of supply increases by more than has been assumed in the example, and/or if the elasticity of demand is lower, then the income of the producers as a group can decrease even if loans are issued exclusively to existing enterprises. Conversely, lending to new entrepreneurs can cause the overall income of producers to increase, provided the loans increase the elasticity of supply only slightly and/or the elasticity of demand is high.

The effect of small loan programmes thus is a function of the price changes they induce. However, while it is easy at a theoretical level to derive the impacts of lending programmes on prices, it is nearly impossible to verify the results of such analyses empirically, as the effects on prices are usually obscured by other effects, making it extremely difficult to isolate and quantify them with any precision. Thus, it is quite possible that although the introduction of credit programmes will lead, overall, to a reduction in incomes in the regions in which they operate, we will still be able to "prove" that such programmes make a positive contribution to combating poverty because, as we have seen, they enable their customers to earn higher incomes.

b) Income growth as a function of previous income levels

We will now endeavour to corroborate the theoretical results derived in the preceding section with data drawn from an empirical study conducted by HULME/MOSLEY.[66] This study investigates the direct impact of credit programmes on borrowers' incomes as a function of previous income levels. In the following, it is assumed that borrowers whose income was previously low are "new entrepreneurs" – i.e., that they were previously unemployed or underemployed. "Existing entrepreneurs" are assumed to have had a somewhat higher income level prior to becoming customers of a credit programme.

---

66 Cf. HULME/MOSLEY, 1996, p. 180-94.

The theoretical analysis presented in preceding section, which took into account the effects of small-scale lending on the relevant markets, showed that if small-scale lending activities achieve a relatively high degree of market penetration, the incomes of new entrepreneurs will show only a slight increase. These absolute increases will not be distributed completely evenly amongst the members of the group of new entrepreneurs, and thus, because the overall effect will be quite small, even moderate variations may cause some enterprises to incur losses. The less capable enterprises are of adapting to changes in the overall economic environment, the greater will be the probability that lending will have an adverse effect on income. There will be a positive correlation between the ability to adapt to changing circumstances and the amount of business experience a given entrepreneur has had, and thus there will presumably also be a positive correlation between an entrepreneur's ability to adapt and his or her income level. According to this line of reasoning, losses in income will thus be incurred above all by the poorest of the poor. By contrast, our analysis has shown that the income-related effect on existing enterprises is relatively pronounced, so that even if there are variations within this group, (nearly) all borrowers should be able to increase their incomes.

In fact, in their empirical study, HULME AND MOSLEY arrive at the conclusion that increases in income, expressed as a percentage of borrowers' previous income levels, are positively correlated with those previous levels. The resulting functional relationships between increases in income and income level for five small loan programmes are depicted in Figure 55. The diagram clearly shows that borrowers whose income was below the poverty line prior to receiving credit (new entrepreneurs) increased their income only slightly, or even earned less than before.

On the basis of these results, we can conclude that it is perhaps not such a good idea after all to attempt to help the poorest of the poor by obliging them to become self-employed. A lack of business experience and management capabilities makes it very difficult for *this* target group to increase their income significantly through self-employment. After all, in industrialised countries, one would not expect persons who are receiving welfare benefits to become successful entrepreneurs!

Instead, small-scale lending should focus on established entrepreneurs. These borrowers already have the know-how needed to run a business, so that cheaper financing options in fact lower costs and eliminate constraints to growth. Provision of less expensive credit to this target group not only has the direct effect of increasing the incomes of the borrowers; in addition, it indirectly helps to increase the wages – and thus the incomes – of the poorest of the poor by creating new jobs in existing enterprises (see Chapter IV.2). By contrast, an approach which focuses too narrowly on "helping the poor", i.e. one which stipulates that the target group of small-scale lending activities should be limited to those who are especially needy, is, as we have shown, counterproductive and serves only to exacerbate poverty.

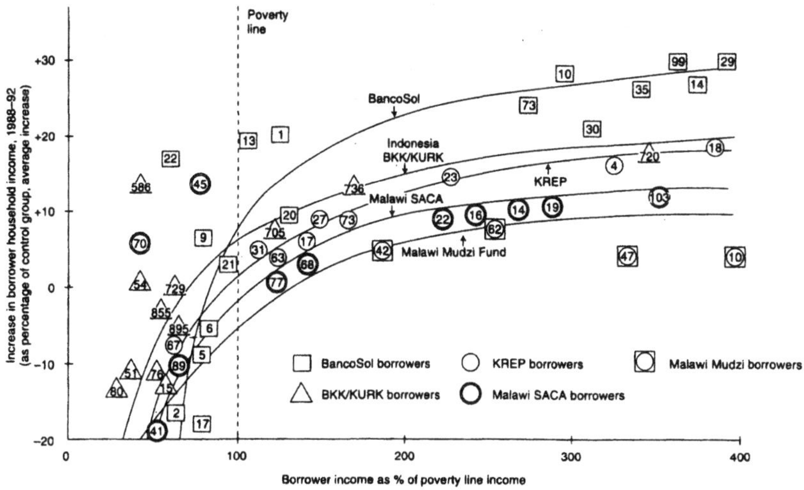

Fig. 55: Increases in income as a function of previous income level
Source: HULME/MOSLEY, 1996, p 184.

4. Impacts at the macro level

This chapter analyses the effects of small-scale lending on the economy as a whole. In particular, it takes a look at how small-scale lending can affect a country's terms of trade, and how this in turn impacts social welfare. The analysis differentiates between the situation faced by a "small country" with constant terms of trade and that of a "large country" with variable terms of trade. It is assumed that large countries must contend with an inelastic demand function, a situation which can affect either individual regions of one country that sell their "export products" in the nearest large city, or the "group of developing countries" which sell similar products to industrialised countries. Throughout most of the following discussion, we will assume the existence of free trade; not until the end of this chapter will this assumption be suspended so as to permit an examination of the ways in which trade-policy instruments could be used to improve welfare, the practicability of these instruments, and the ways in which successful implementation of small-scale lending activities affects the feasibility of using such instruments.

Free trade can be said to exist only if trading profits can be realised. To illustrate this point, a trade indifference curve (TI) has been derived in Figure 56. A region or a country (referred to in the following as the "domestic economy") can produce combinations of goods M and X in keeping with its production possibility frontier(PPF). The indifference curve "I" reflects the society's preferences with respect to the consumption of these goods; the utility of consumption is the same for all points on this function. Shifting the production possibility frontierupwards along the indifference curve yields a set of points in the quadrant that represents the foreign trade market; by connecting these points, we obtain the trade indifference curve "TI", which, for a given export quantity of good X, shows how much of good M must be imported to ensure that the level of social welfare will not change.[67]

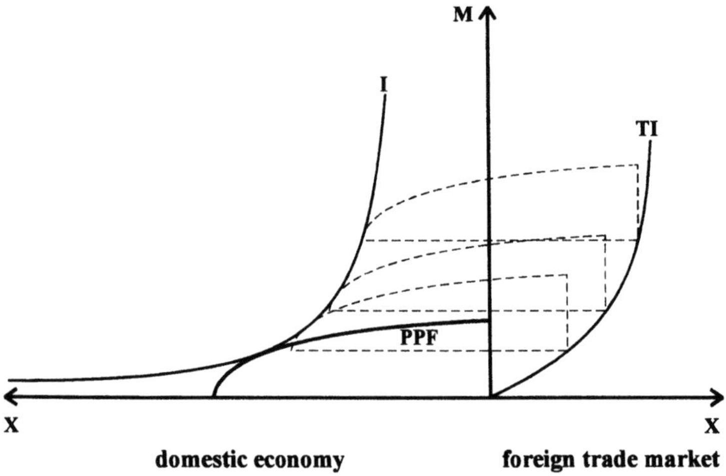

Fig. 56: The derivation of the trade indifference curve

Thus, if a given trade transaction were located precisely on the trade indifference curve, the society would be indifferent as to whether this transaction should be carried out or not. However, we have already asserted that trade will only take place if trading profits can be realised, i.e. if the level of social welfare increases as a result of trade transactions. Figure 57 depicts the indifference curve introduced in the preceding diagram (now I^1), as well as four additional indifference curves (I^2 – I^5), each of which corresponds to a higher level of welfare that cannot be attained without trade. It is assumed that the demand for good M is income-elastic, while the demand for good X is income-inelastic. Shifting the production possibility frontierupwards along the indifference curves I^2 – I^5 yields trade indifference curves TI^2 to TI^5.

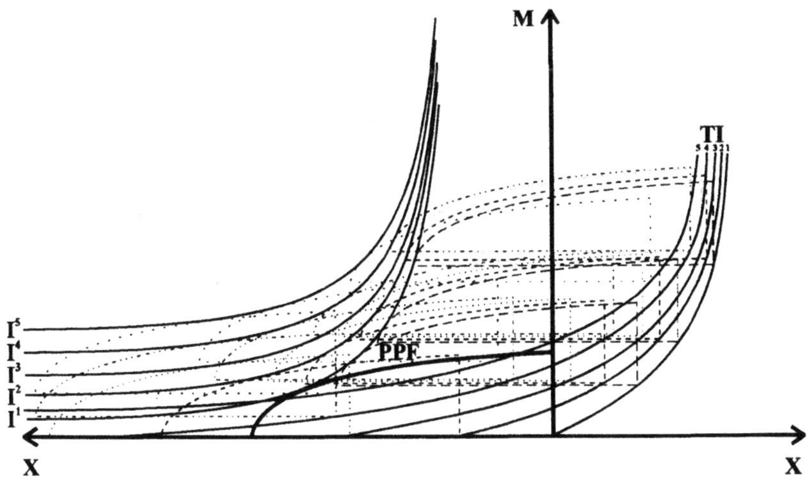

Fig. 57: The derivation of a family of indifference curves

For example, if the domestic economy can trade on TI^5, social welfare equivalent to I^5 can be attained. Yet, at which point on this curve will the domestic economy choose to trade, and is it in fact free to choose a point on the curve? To answer this question, we will first examine the situation of small countries. In a small country, the domestic economy is a price taker in the foreign trade market, and prices are determined exogenously. Figure 58 shows five possible prices which have been determined exogenously, and the resulting adjustment which takes place in response to these prices. Given a price ratio which corresponds to terms of trade 1 (ToT^1), the maximum level of welfare that this country could attain – without any trade taking place – is I^1. However, a moderate increase in prices (to ToT^2) will be enough to enhance the level of welfare without trade, welfare will again not exceed I^1, but now trade can also

67 For the derivation of the trade indifference curve, cf. ROSE, 1989, p. 382.

take place at the point of tangency between ToT^2 and TI^2, for example, causing welfare to rise to I^2.

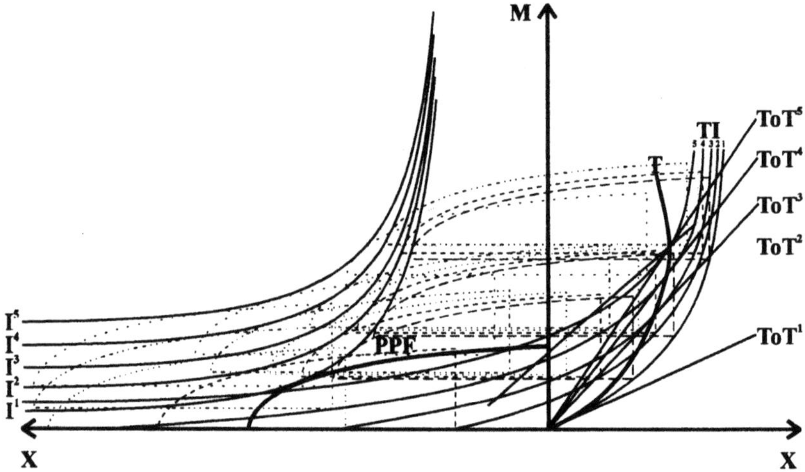

Fig. 58: The derivation of the trade curve

For given terms of trade, welfare will always be maximised if trade takes place at the point of tangency between the trade indifference curve and the ToT line. Otherwise, welfare can be further optimised through an improved process of adjustment in the domestic economy, and thus the domestic economy will only engage in trade at points of tangency. The "trade curve" (T) is the line which connects these optimal points, and thus it determines the precise nature of the trade in which the domestic economy will engage for each specific price ratio indicated by the various terms of trade lines.

Demand for the exports of a small country will be completely elastic. If, for example, terms of trade represented by ToT^4 have emerged in the foreign trade market, any given quantity can be traded at this price ratio. The terms of trade line is then identical to the trade curve of the foreign economy.

A large country is faced with a different situation – namely, there is a negative correlation between the price and the export quantity. Figure 59 depicts a possible price/sales function (foreign demand). Let us assume that, in total, the world market for good M is much larger than the quantity imported by the domestic economy, and that the selling price of this good therefore does not vary in response to fluctuations in demand in the domestic market. In this case, the trade curve for the foreign economy can be derived with the help of a simplified procedure based on the price/sales function for exported good X.[68]

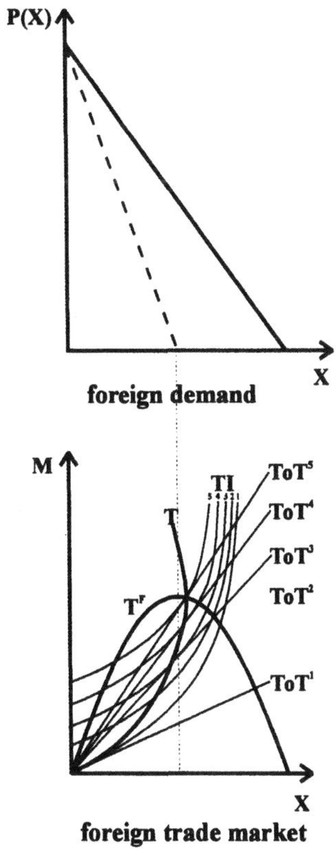

Fig. 59: The trade curve of the foreign economy

If trade takes place at the points where the price/sales function intersects one of the axes, there will be no export earnings, i.e. no goods at all can be imported. Between these points, the country can import good M in accordance with the trade curve for the foreign market (T^F). Given free trade, trade will occur at the point where the two trade curves intersect; in other words, terms of trade 5 will emerge. As a result, trade indifference curve 5 will apply to the domestic economy, and the level of social welfare it achieves will rise to I^5.

68 The curve obtained via this simplified derivation is not qualitatively different from the trade curve yielded by a traditional derivation.

This brief summary of traditional foreign trade theory can now be used to describe how efficient small-scale lending impacts social welfare. In keeping with the results obtained in IV.2, it is assumed in Figure 60 that small-scale lending will enable the domestic economy to produce more of its export commodity. The production possibility frontieris extended to the left along the axis representing good X. If the indifference curves for domestic consumption all remain unchanged, welfare level I^2 will be attained even in the absence of trade. In this example as well, the trade indifference curves TI^2 to TI^5 and the resulting new trade curve, T', have been derived.

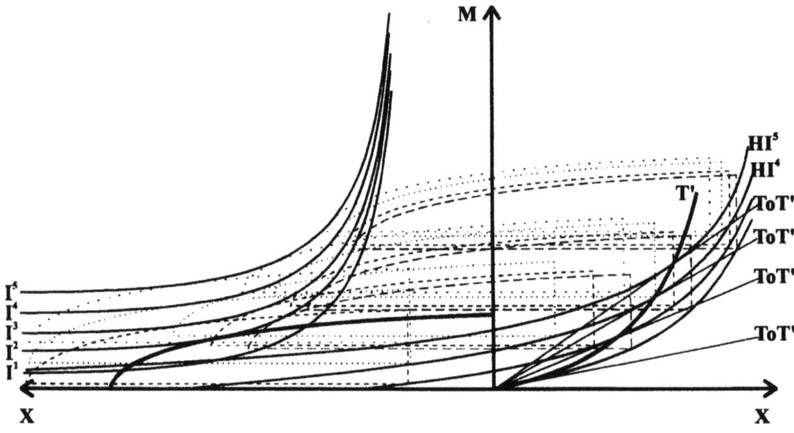

Fig. 60: The trade curve given efficient small-scale lending

Figure 61 directly compares the situation prior to and following the introduction of small-scale lending; the trade curve has shifted downwards and to the right. In the case of the small country depicted here, small-scale lending clearly has a positive impact on welfare, as higher trade indifference curves will be attained for all possible price ratios. In the diagram, this phenomenon is depicted for a price ratio of ToT'^4. Without small loans, consumption is limited to X^0 and M^0, and the maximum possible level of welfare will be just slightly higher than I^1; however, if small-scale lending is successfully introduced, consumption will increase to X' and M', in turn boosting welfare to I^4. If the terms of trade are determined exogenously, small-scale lending enables a country to achieve a higher level of social welfare than it would have if small loans were not available. Put another way, without small-scale lending the terms of trade would have to be significantly more favourable to attain the same level of welfare (ToT^4). Therefore, for a small country the introduction of efficient small-scale lending is without a doubt a sensible approach.

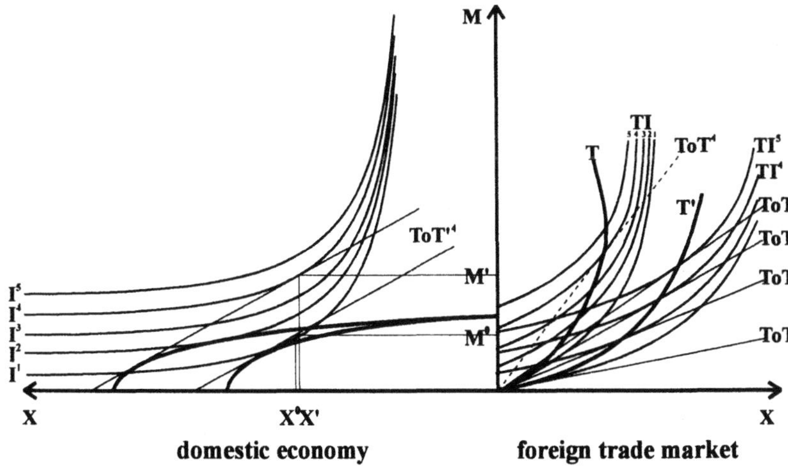

Fig. 61: The trade curve prior to and following the introduction of small-scale lending

This is not necessarily true for large countries, however. Figure 62 shows an enlarged, more detailed view of the international market under the conditions assumed above. We have already seen that, given the existence of free trade, trade takes place at the point(s) where the terms of trade are tangent to the trade indifference curve. As shown above, prior to the introduction of small-scale lending trade takes place on trade curve T at terms of trade 5, yielding trade indifference curve TI^5; this in turn enables the country to attain a welfare level of I^5. Following the implementation of small-scale lending, the trade curve shifts to the position represented by T', causing the terms of trade to deteriorate considerably (ToT'^{4}). Consequently, the country's trade indifference curve will shift downward to TI^4, and thus its welfare level will decrease slightly to I^4.

Therefore, efficient small-scale lending which leads to an increase in the production of export goods can cause the terms of trade to deteriorate and even lead to a lower level of social welfare. Whether this situation will in fact materialise depends on the various elasticities of supply and demand. The more elastic the supply of the exported product is, the less income-elastic domestic demand for the same good is, and the more inelastic the export demand or the trade curve of the international market is, the greater will be the likelihood of a decline in the level of social welfare; and the greater will be the extent of the resulting welfare loss should such a loss occur. In fact, the supply of many products produced in poor regions is highly elastic, while domestic demand for these goods exhibits a low degree of income-elasticity and export demand is highly inelastic as well. And this is why successful small loan programmes may well serve to exacerbate poverty in these regions.

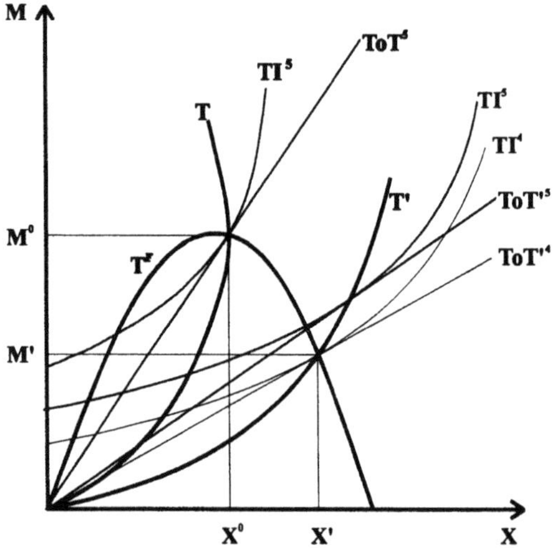

foreign trade market

Fig. 62: The impact of an efficient small-scale lending programme on the international trade market of a large country

At this juncture, it must again be emphasised that regions as a whole can become poorer even as the incomes of the customers of small loan programmes in those regions rise. For this reason, superficial impact analyses which capture only the direct income effects of small loans conclude that small-scale lending is an effective instrument for fighting poverty in an increasingly complex world in which the problem of wide-scale economic marginalisation seems ever more difficult to address. For one individual region which competes with other regions and must act as a price taker in its market, this conclusion is certainly justified. However, this is not the case if we broaden the focus of our analysis to cover the "group" of all regions. If small-scale lending is successful in all regions, then the supply of a given good produced for export will increase everywhere; if the overall demand for this product is inelastic, the price will show a disproportionate decline and the welfare level will decrease in all regions.

We will now analyse whether instruments of trade policy can be used to enhance domestic welfare, and if so, how this might be done. It is assumed that the production possibility frontierwould correspond to that derived for the situation following the introduction of small-scale lending as depicted above in Fig. 61. Figure 63 shows that, if the foreign market has a trade curve as shown, the welfare level would increase considerably at a price ratio of ToT^8. However, this situation would not be compatible with the free trade equilibrium that would emerge at the point of intersection of the trade curves, as such an equilibrium would give rise to a price ratio of ToT^4, and in turn create a welfare level of I^4.

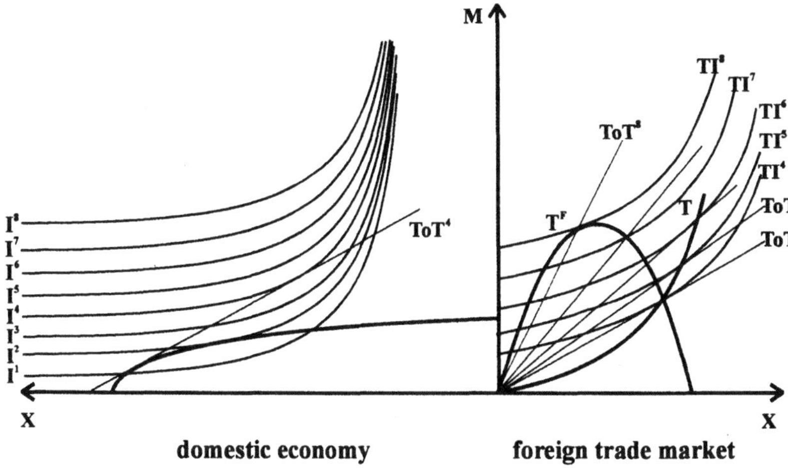

Fig. 63: Increases in the level of welfare in a state of disequilibrium

Thus, implementation of a trade policy that induced the domestic economy to engage in foreign trade at the point of intersection between ToT^8 and T^F could increase the welfare level to I^8. However, external intervention would be needed in order to produce this outcome because, given a price ratio of ToT^8, the demand for good M will exceed by a sizeable margin the supply of this good that is offered in the international market.

To reduce demand, the domestic price of good M would have to increase to ToT^8_I (see Figure 64). The necessary differential between the domestic and foreign price ratios can be created by levying a tariff in the amount of t^{opt} on good M. If such a tariff is imposed, domestic production and consumption will adjust to the new domestic price of ToT^8_I, while good M will continue to be traded in the foreign market at ToT^8. If we assume that the tariff will be levied in units of good M, its imposition will cause the domestic trade curve to be extended upward and to the left, moving from T to T^T,[69] with the quantity X' now being exported at the point where the foreign trade curve and the new trade curve, T^T, intersect so as to permit importation of M'. Of the total amount of goods imported, M', domestic exporters receive M'', and the remainder – i.e. the difference between M' and M'' – corresponds to the tariff paid.

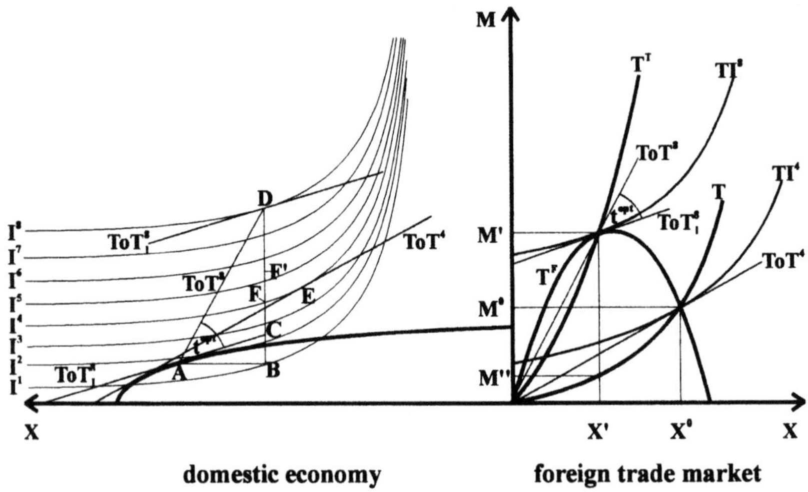

Fig. 64: Increases in welfare through the use of trade-policy instruments

In the domestic economy, less of X and more of M will be produced (Point A) than would be the case under free trade, as producers will adjust to the new price ratio ToT^8_I. Overall, a quantity corresponding to the segment AB (=X') will be exported; in turn, good M is imported in a quantity corresponding to BD (=M') at the foreign trade price of ToT^8. At Point D, consumption, for its part, adjusts to the domestic price ToT^8_I. The tariff has increased the welfare level from I^4 to I^8.

Yet there is some doubt as to whether the trade policy instruments described here could ever actually be implemented. After all, the "group of developing countries" is not *one* large country, but rather comprises many individual producers and suppliers of goods. However, each individual country is a *small* country, and the demand for its exports is completely elastic, which in turn

69 If the tariff were levied in units of good X, this would compress the trade curve toward the y-axis.

means that from the point of view of each individual country it is rational to forgo the imposition of tariffs on its own imports and profit as a free rider from the tariffs levied by other countries, and thus from higher prices in the international markets. Yet if all countries behave as free riders, the trade curve T will remain unchanged, i.e. terms of trade 4 will emerge, leading to a welfare level of I^4. An individual region which "exports" its products to the nearest large city cannot levy tariffs in any case, in other words, it cannot make use of any trade-policy instruments.

This does not, however, render our analysis irrelevant. Although it is scarcely feasible for state institutions in the individual regions or countries to use trade-policy instruments, often this "function of government" is performed – particularly in rural areas – by traders who use their monopolies in the marketing of export goods to earn monopoly profits. They buy good X in the domestic market at a very low price (ToT_I^8), and then sell it in the foreign market at a price which, in comparison with their costs, is disproportionately high (ToT^8). Their monopoly profits correspond to the tariffs derived above. Because traders in the other regions or countries behave in precisely the same manner, the prices and output quantities derived above will emerge (of course, depending on the level of competition, lower prices can also emerge; however, in the following it is assumed that an absolute monopoly exists).

In itself, though, the fact that the traders' monopoly profits have the same effect as the tariff described above, i.e. the fact that they in effect levy this tariff, does not ensure that the other members of society will enjoy greater welfare than they would under conditions of free trade. In the following, the welfare of society as a whole will be equated with the welfare of "non-traders" since the traders' monopoly profits benefit only a very small group of persons who are not, however, the focus of this analysis.

The traders achieve monopoly profits represented by segment CD. Non-traders can consume goods in a quantity that corresponds to point C. In other words, their welfare decreases in comparison with the free trade situation (E), despite the fact that the welfare of the society as a whole has increased. This is because – at least in the case of the primary distribution – the shift from a free trade situation has led to a substantial redistribution of income from the non-traders to the traders.

However, the monopolists are not just traders. If they were, they could easily be replaced by other traders, and the ensuing competition would eliminate their monopoly rents. These traders are able to maintain their monopolies because, via "patronage systems", they provide their customers with additional services such as loans and transfers in emergencies.[70] Thus, part of the traders' surplus is distributed back to the non-traders. And if the amount of the surplus that is redistributed is equivalent to segment CF, this will already be sufficient to enable the non-traders to achieve the same level of welfare as they would under free trade. If the traders distribute half of their monopoly profits to their customers (segment CF'), the welfare of the non-traders will increase significantly beyond this level (i.e. significantly beyond the level attainable under free trade). Monopolistic "patronage systems" can thus lead to welfare gains for the society as a whole.

Monopolistic "patronage systems" are based on a relationship of dependency between the client and the patron. This dependency is typically established through credit relationships; however, the credit relationships that form the basis of "patronage systems" are undermined by the introduction of small-loan programmes, as loans granted by the new programmes take the place of the informal loans provided by the "patrons". This erodes the power of the "patrons", who, as a consequence, are also forced to relinquish their monopolies because the producers who have so far been their clients are now free to sell their goods to whomever they like. Consequently, competition among those who market their output intensifies, and this causes the monopoly profits of the traders to decline, perhaps to the point where they are eliminated altogether. A trend toward free trade emerges in the foreign market, the terms of trade deteriorate, and the welfare of the society as a whole decreases.

Efficient small-scale lending can thus diminish or even destroy the power of the "patrons", undermining their monopolies. At the same time, this can also diminish their clients' welfare, in particular if the "patrons" were formerly in a position to use their power to prevent any major declines in the price of goods exported by the domestic economy in a foreign market with inelastic demand.

---

70 For a detailed description of "patronage systems", cf. TSCHACH, 1995, p. 31-39.

Summary and Conclusions

If, owing to information asymmetries, it is difficult for banks to assess accurately whether specific entrepreneurs are able and/or willing to pay, implicit interest rate ceilings will emerge. Although the maximum interest rate increases as the size of enterprises decreases, such ceilings nonetheless constrain the banks' ability to set interest rates at a level that would enable them to cover costs. If transaction costs are high, the total costs associated with granting small and medium-sized loans will exceed the maximum average return which the banks can earn by issuing such loans. For this reason, banks do not lend to small and medium-sized enterprises, and, as a consequence, these businesses have no access to formal loans (I.1 – I.3).

Because micro and small enterprises have a very high RoI, it is worthwhile for them to rely on expensive informal loans to finance their operations, at least until they reach a certain size. Once they have reached this size, however, it does not make economic sense for them to continue taking out informal credits, and thus they face a growth constraint imposed by the credit market. Internally financed growth does not take place because, given the entrepreneurs' high rates of time preference, surplus funds are used for other purposes, i.e. allocated to finance alternative investments or expenditures. Medium-sized enterprises earn a lower RoI than small ones, which is why borrowing in the informal credit market is not a worthwhile option for them. Moreover, they do not have access to credit from formal financial institutions, and are thus excluded from obtaining any kind of financing in either of the two credit markets. The credit market is segmented (I.4).

The inability to access credit is a significant competitive disadvantage. For this reason, the size distribution of enterprises in "developing countries" is characterised by a "missing middle", i.e. there are hardly any medium-sized enterprises (II.1). Because small enterprises finance their activities with expensive informal loans, their RoI must be correspondingly high, which in turn means that their operations must be highly labour-intensive. As a result, the wage level in the informal sector is low. By contrast, large enterprises have access to relatively inexpensive formal loans, enabling them to employ capital-intensive production methods, which in turn leads to high labour productivity and permits them to pay comparatively high wages. Although the high wages in the formal sector attract more labour than this sector can absorb, employees in this sector are able to form effective organisations (unions) to ensure that wages do not drop. In addition, the high labour productivity enables employers to pay high wages, which the same time lessens the effects of information asymmetries between employers and employees. For these reasons, employers have no incentives to reduce wages. Thus, the labour market, like the credit market, is segmented (II.2).

Segmentation in the labour and credit markets causes factor price differentials to arise between the formal and informal sectors, and thus leads to various factor input intensities. The intensity of factor utilisation does not reflect the shadow prices that are valid for the economy as a whole, resulting in static efficiency losses. Dynamic efficiency losses occur on the one hand because the constraints to growth faced by small enterprises prevent the formation of a broad-based "entrepreneurial class", and on the other because it is more difficult for enterprises to adapt to changing conditions in the overall economic environment (II.3). Factor market segmentation results not only in efficiency losses, but also in a more uneven distribution of income (II.4). Despite these disadvantages, the system is stable in politico-economic terms (II.5).

If factor segmentation and its adverse effects are to be eliminated, then credit rationing on the basis of enterprise size must be largely eliminated. However, the credit technology that has traditionally been used by banks makes it impossible for them to lend to small and medium-sized enterprises; therefore, instruments must be found which can solve the problems described in Part I. A mere increase in the propensity to save will not be sufficient to eliminate credit rationing (III.2).

Banks often find it difficult to assess the potential borrowers' willingness to pay. Problems in this area can be solved or circumvented if the bank carries out a cash flow-oriented credit analysis of the entire family economic unit of the small entrepreneur and provides potential borrowers with intertemporal incentives to ensure that they have a vested interest in ensuring that their loans are repaid on time. A reduction in the lending bank's transaction costs (and thus a lowering of its interest rates) will also have a positive effect, as will an improvement in the overall economic situation (III.3).

Borrowers' willingness to pay depends not only on their mentality and attitude toward credit, but is also influenced by cultural aspects and the social distance between those who take out loans and the institution from which they borrow. Peer pressure can be brought to bear as one way of increasing the willingness to pay. Moreover, if it becomes less expensive for credit institutions to enforce their legal claims, they will have a greater incentive to recover non-performing loans, and this will, in turn, tend to make their customers more willing to meet their obligations. The costs of enforcing legal claims can be reduced by changing the relevant legislation. However, banks can also lower their loan-recovery costs by permitting borrowers to pledge household goods with a high utility value as collateral that will be seized if they fall behind in their payments. Depending on the legal environment, another option is to have the borrower write a post-dated cheque for each instalment. In itself, the expectation on the part of the borrower that the lending institution will make every effort to enforce its claims will lead to a decisive increase in his or her willingness to pay (III.4).

There are three institutional approaches to small-scale lending, namely group credit programmes, individual credit programmes, and small-scale lending via existing banks (downscaling). Group credit programmes are usually geared towards alleviating poverty, i.e. they grant loans primarily to the poorest of the poor. They have competitive advantages in this segment of the market, above all in rural regions, because their credit technology involves having the borrowers assume responsibility for tasks whose execution would normally cost the programme money (monitoring and enforcing repayment). For this reason, they are better able to grant very small loans than are small-scale lending projects which employ one of the other two approaches. At the same time, however, their credit technology requires a significant input of time by the borrowers. However, the fact that borrowing from group lending programmes is time-consuming is not a problem for the customers of such programmes, at least at the beginning. As many people are either unemployed or underemployed when they join group programmes, the opportunity costs of their time are quite low, and they receive valuable insurance services along with the loans in return for devoting time to the group borrowing process. However, group credit programmes usually contribute little to reducing factor market segmentation or narrowing the structural gap in the size distribution of enterprises (III.5.a).

Individual credit programmes have explicitly set themselves the goal of deepening the financial market, i.e. their objective is to reduce or eliminate credit market segmentation. They lend primarily to existing enterprises that previously had no access to formal credits. This approach is intended to close the structural gap in the credit market and enable small enterprises to grow into the medium size range, and around 1% of the large number of micro and small enterprises that use the services of individual loan programmes – a not inconsiderable share of the total – manage to achieve growth on this scale.[71] Over the long term, this can close the gap in the size distribution of enterprises. Extremely poor people are not served by individual credit programmes, yet they profit indirectly from the creation of new jobs in which labour can be employed

---

[71] Cf. LIEDHOLM/MEAD, 1998, p. 7.

more productively, which in turn increases wage rates in the informal sector (III.5.b).

By granting targeted subsidies in conjunction with downscaling programmes, development agencies can induce banks to grant small loans. As a rule, the banks that participate in downscaling activities serve a segment of the enterprise sector that is slightly closer to the top end of the market than the target group of individual credit programmes, although they use the same credit technology. Because banks can utilise their existing branch networks, lending can get under way on a significant scale within a relatively short time. However, banks will always have an incentive to pocket the subsidies without actually granting small loans. It is expensive to monitor the intermediaries that take part in downscaling programmes, which is why the suitability of this institutional alternative must be determined on a case-by-case basis (III.5.c).

The financial sector can profit from small-scale lending if individual credit programmes grant loans not only to micro and small enterprises, but also to medium-sized businesses. This serves to close the structural gap in the credit market "from below". Banks can close the gap "from above" by lending to larger small enterprises and medium-sized businesses. By contrast, group credit programmes are at most a useful supplement to the two other options. The closure of the gap in the credit market will, over the long term, enable the segmentation of the size distribution of enterprises (the problem of the "missing middle") to be eliminated as well (IV.1).

Efficient small-scale lending that does not attempt to suspend the laws of the market will always cause activity in the production sector to increase disproportionately. The fear that the provision of small loans will benefit only traders, i.e. lead only to growth in the trade sector, is unfounded. In fact, the trade sector will most likely contract, at least over the medium-to-long term; and if it does expand, its growth will be disproportionately small compared with that of the production sector. At the same time, efficient small-scale lending causes wages in the informal sector to increase and reduces labour market segmentation (IV.2).

If an impact analysis of small-scale lending also takes into account its indirect effects, i.e. how small-scale lending affects the market, it can be expected to show that the income effects are double-edged. Although borrowers' incomes will increase, the small enterprises that did not receive small loans will suffer income losses. The lower the elasticity of demand for the products produced by small enterprises, and the more the elasticity of supply increases as a result of the introduction of small-scale lending, the more pronounced these income losses will be. Granting loans to extremely poor people has at best only a slight positive effect on the income of borrowers and non-borrowers, and it may even have a negative impact on incomes in both groups (IV.3).

The successful introduction of small-scale lending in many different regions or countries that sell their products in the same market can lead to a deterioration in the terms of trade of those regions or countries, and thus to social welfare losses in the economies that are involved. The lower the elasticity of demand – both in the domestic and the export markets – and the higher the elasticity of supply, the greater will be the likelihood of this outcome. And in many sectors that receive small loans, the elasticity of demand is low while the elasticity of supply is high, which is why small-scale lending should always be accompanied by an active structural policy that encourages enterprises to seek new markets where the elasticity of demand is higher, and supports them in adapting their production activities to the requirements of these new markets. Without such a strategy, small-scale lending will still be a worthwhile option from the point of view of each individual country or region, but the welfare of the group of all countries or regions that sell their products in the market in question will decline (IV.4).

This study is the first to identify and discuss all of the impacts of small-scale lending programmes. It shows that their positive impacts far exceed the beneficial effects that have heretofore been attributed to such programmes, at least with respect to individual credit programmes and downscaling projects. They are not only capable of enhancing their customers' incomes, eliminating credit market segmentation, and reducing the constraints to growth faced by small businesses; they also reduce the extent of segmentation in the size distribution of enterprises and in the labour market. Income distribution is made more even, not only because borrowers' incomes increase, but also because wage levels in the informal sector rise. Moreover, the economy as a whole functions more efficiently, in turn promoting further growth.

However, if small-scale lending programmes achieve a significant outreach, negative effects can also be expected. In particular, if demand for the goods produced by small enterprises – the output of which will increase as a result of small-scale lending – is inelastic, prices will drop disproportionately, which is why enterprises that do not receive credit will suffer losses in income. The terms of trade can deteriorate to the point that the welfare of the society as a whole declines. If a process of structural adjustment cannot be rapidly carried out in the informal sector, small loan programmes can turn out to have a negative overall impact.

Nonetheless, it makes sense to implement small-scale credit programmes. It can be expected that the positive effects will more than compensate for the negative ones, especially since the latter can be alleviated if targeted measures are implemented to promote structural adjustment in the small enterprise sector.

Development agencies should focus more on four key tasks: Firstly, individual credit programmes and downscaling projects need to receive more support; at the same time, subsidies to group credit programmes should continue to be reduced. There are a number of reasons for this. Specifically, individual credit programmes and downscaling projects have the following advantages over group credit programmes in that they:

- rely less on subsidies, and thus exhibit a higher degree of institutional stability over the long term;
- have more pronounced direct income effects because these effects are positively correlated with the original income level of the borrowers, and because individual credit programmes and downscaling projects serve the segment of the market consisting of the "more affluent" poor;
- induce stronger growth effects, since larger small enterprises achieve a higher level of labour productivity;[72]
- are capable of reducing or even eliminating credit market segmentation, which means that they in turn reduce the degree of segmentation in the size distribution of enterprises and in the labour market, increase the efficiency of the economy as a whole, and promote the emergence of a broader-based entrepreneurial class;
- serve a segment of the target group that is more likely to be able to undertake structural adjustments.

Moreover, from an institutional standpoint these programmes have a greater potential to develop a sustainable supply of complementary products (see below).

Secondly, development assistance organisations should set themselves the task of supporting the further refinement and practical testing of new or improved financial technologies. Support in this area would serve to enable development finance institutions to reduce their costs, as well as improve and expand their range of products over the medium term. Over the long term, the target group should be offered the full range of financial services that it requires, which includes insurance services in addition to typical banking services such as domestic payment transactions and foreign transfers. When it comes to providing insurance services, target group-oriented financial institutions have competitive advantages: they are characterised by a high degree of social

---

72 Cf. LIEDHOLM/MEAD, 1998, p. 4.

proximity to the target group; they have already established credit relationships with their customers that have enabled them to reduce information asymmetries; and they can realise economies of scope by being active in both markets simultaneously. All measures geared to introducing improved financial technologies should be carried out with the goal of making the services offered to the target group increasingly profitable for the partner institutions. Indeed, the long-term objective here must be to achieve a level of profitability in serving small enterprises that is high enough to eventually make this clientele an attractive market segment for purely profit-oriented banks as well. When this point is reached, small entrepreneurs will find that their demand for financial services can be satisfied in competitive markets.

Thirdly, development institutions should use the strong negotiating position they have in "developing countries" to improve the overall operating environment for target group-oriented financial institutions. In most cases, the banking laws of these countries have been designed to provide a regulatory framework for traditional banks, and in a number of respects they are not suited to the needs of small-scale lenders. Indeed, in some instances the existing legislation may make it very difficult for local financial institutions to develop the small loan market. Moreover, laws which clearly favour debtors at the expense of creditors, providing an excessive degree of protection to the former, should be revised or eliminated altogether.

Finally, development agencies should furnish targeted support to promote structural adjustment in the small enterprise sector. Without such support, small-scale lending may prove to be counterproductive, as it cannot be expected that micro and small enterprises will be capable on their own of identifying and developing new markets for their output in which demand is more elastic. If they were able to develop new markets on their own, they would have already done so, and they would also have already made the changes to their operations needed to enable them to produce for such markets. Thus, development institutions must promote structural adjustment to ensure that the great potential presented by small-scale lending can indeed be realised.

Literature

ADAMS, DALE W. and GRAHAM, DOUGLAS H. (1981): A Critique of Traditional Agricultural Credit Projects and Policies, *in: Journal of Development Economics, Vol. 8, 1981, pp. 347-366.*

ADAMS, DALE W., GRAHAM, DOUGLAS H. and VON PISCHKE, J.D. (Eds.) (1984): Undermining Rural Development with Cheap Credit, Boulder.

BELL, CLIVE (1988): Credit Markets and Interlinked Transactions, *in: CHENERY, H. and SRINIVASAN, T.N. (Eds.): Handbook of Development Economics, Vol. I, 1988, pp. 763-830.*

BMZ (1994): Sektorkonzept Finanzsystementwicklung – Förderung von Sparen und Kredit, Bonn.

CAMARA, M. (1998): Die Finanzsektorreform in Afrika – Das Beispiel der Franc-Zone, Frankfurt.

GILLIS, M., PERKINS, D.H., ROEMER, M. and SNODGRASS, D.R. (1987): Economics of Development, Second Edition, London.

GONZÁLEZ-VEGA, C. (1984): Credit-Rationing Behavior of Agricultural Lenders: The Iron Law of Interest Rate Restrictions, *in: ADAMS, D.W., GRAHAM, D.H., VON PISCHKE, J.D. (Eds.): Undermining Rural Development with Cheap Credit, Boulder.*

GONZÁLEZ-VEGA, C. (1996): Microfinanzas en El Salvador – Lecciones y Perspectivas, Fundación Manuel Ungo, San Salvador.

GONZÁLEZ-VEGA, C. SCHREINER, M. NAVAJAS, S., RODRÍGUEZ-MEZA, J., MEYER, R.L. (1997): A Primer on Bolivian Experiences in Microfinance: An Ohio State Perspective, Rural Finance Program, Ohio State University, Columbus.

GREENWALD, B.C. and STIGLITZ, J.E. (1987): Imperfect Information, Credit Markets and Unemployment, *in: European Economic Review 31, 1987, pp. 444-456.*

HECKSCHER, E. (1919): The Effect of Foreign Trade on the Distribution of Income, Economisk Tidskrift, Bd. 21, 1919.

HULME, D. and MOSLEY, P. (1996a): Finance against Poverty, Vol. 1, London.

JACKELEN, HENRY R. and RHYNE, ELISABETH (1991): Toward a More Market Orientated Approach to Credit and Savings for the Poor. Mimeo, Washington.

JAIN, P.S. (1997): Managing Fast Expansion of Micro-Credit Programs (The Lessons from ASA), Dhaka.

KRAHNEN, JAN-PIETER and SCHMIDT, REINHARD H. (1994): Development Finance as Institution Building – A New Approach to Poverty-Oriented Banking, Boulder.

LEADHOLM, C. and MEAD, D. (1993): The Structure and Growth of Microenterprises in Southern and Eastern Africa: Evidence from Recent Surveys, Michigan State University.

LEADHOLM, C. and MEAD, D. (1998): The Dynamics of Micro and Small Enterprises in Developing Countries, *in: World Development, Jan. 1998.*

LEPP, A. (1997): The "making" of Calpiá and Los Andes, Vortrag auf dem *First Annual Seminar on New Development Finance,* Frankfurt.

LIPTON, MICHAEL (1976): Agricultural Finance and Rural Credit in Poor Countries, *in: World Development, Vol. 4, No. 7, 1976, pp. 543-553.*

MCKINNON, RONALD I. (1973): Money and Capital in Economic Development, Washington, D.C..

NELSON, BENJAMIN (1969): The Idea of Usury. From Tribal Brotherhood to Universal Otherhood, Chicago.

NITSCH, M., SCHMIDT, R.H. und ZEITINGER, C.-P. (1981): Die entwicklungspolitische Wirksamkeit der Förderung von Entwicklungsbanken in Lateinamerika, Gutachten für das BMZ, Bonn.

OHLIN, B. (1931): Die Beziehungen zwischen internationalem Handel und internationalen Bewegungen von Kapital und Arbeit, *in: Zeitschrift für Nationalökonomie, Bd. 2, 1931.*

OLSON, M. (1968): Die Logik kollektiven Handelns, Tübingen.

PEEGE, FRIEDRICH-KARL (1988): Die Grameen Bank in Bangladesh - ein Vorbild für die Sparkassentätigkeit in der Dritten Welt, *in: Sparkasse, 105. Jahrgang, Nr. 4, 1988, pp. 166-168.*

ROSE, K. (1989): Theorie der Außenwirtschaft, 10. Auflage, München.

RYBCZYNSKI, T.M. (1955): Factor Endowment and Relative Commodity Prices, *in: Economica N.S., Bd. 22, 1955.*

SAMUELSON, P.A. (1948): International Trade and the Equalization of Factor Prices, *in: Economic Journal, Vol. 58, 1948.*

SAMUELSON, P.A. (1949): International Factor-price Equlization Once Again, *in: Economic Journal, Vol. 59, 1949.*

SAMUELSON, P.A. (1953-54): Prices of Factors and Goods in General Equilibrium, *in: Review of Economic Studies, Vol. 21, 1953-54.*

SAMUELSON, P.A. (1967): Summary on Factor-Price Equalization, *in: International Economic Review, Vol 8, 1967.*

SCHMIDT, R.H. and MOMMARTZ, R. (1996): A strategy for the IDB/El Salvador in the area of financial services for micro-enterprises, Vol. 1: The Strategy, Vol. 2: Appendices, IPC Frankfurt.

SCHMIDT, R.H. and ZEITINGER, C.-P. (1994): Critical Issues in Small and Microbusiness Finance, IPC Frankfurt.

SCHMIDT, R.H. and ZEITINGER, C.-P. (1996): Prospects, Problems and Potential of Credit-Granting NGO's, *in: Journal of International Development, Vol. 8, No. 2, 1996, pp. 241-258.*

SCHMIDT, R.H. and ZEITINGER, C.-P. (1998): Critical Issues in Microbusiness Finance and the Role of Donors, *in: KIMENYI, M.S., WIELAND, R.C., VON PISCHKE, J.D. (Eds.): Strategic Issues in Microfinance, Vermont.*

SHAPIRO, C. and STIGLITZ, JOSEPH E. (1984): Equilibrium Unemployment as a Worker Discipline Device, *in: The American Economic Review, Vol. 74, No. 3, June 1984, pp. 433-444.*

SHAW, E.S. (1973): Financial Deepening in Economic Development, New York.

SIMON, H.A. (1993): Homo Rationalis - Die Vernunft im menschlichen Leben, Frankfurt.

STIGLITZ, JOSEPH E. (1985): Equilibrium Wage Distributions, *in: The Economic Journal, Vol. 95, Sept. 1985, pp. 595-618.*

STIGLITZ, JOSEPH E. and WEISS, ANDREW (1981): Credit Rationing in Markets with Imperfect Information, *in: American Economic Review, Vol. 71, No. 3, June 1981, pp. 393-410.*

STIGLITZ, JOSEPH E. and WEISS, ANDREW (1983): Incentive Effects of Terminations: Applications to the Credit and Labor Markets, *in: American Economic Review, Vol. 73, No. 5, December 1983, pp. 912-927.*

STOLPER, W.F. and SAMUELSON, P.A. (1941): Protection and Real Wages, *in: Review of Economic Studies, Vol. 9, 1941.*

TIMBERG, T.A. and AIYAR, C.V. (1984): Informal Credit Markets in India, *in: Economic Development and Cultural Change, Vol. 33, No. 1, Oct. 1984, pp. 43-59.*

TRENK, MARIN (1991): Der Schatten der Verschuldung: komplexe Kreditbeziehungen des informellen Finanzsektors, Saarbrücken.

TSCHACH, I. (1995): Kleinkredite als Mittel zur Armutsbekämpfung? Möglichkeiten, Grenzen und Alternativen zur Schaffung einer funktionierenden Finanzintermediation, *Diskussionsbeitrag Nr. 67 des Ibero-Amerika-Instituts für Wirtschaftsforschung, Göttingen.*

VOGEL, ROBERT C. (1984): The Effect of Subsidized Agricultural Credit on Income Distribution in Costa Rica, *in: ADAMS, DALE W., GRAHAM, DOUGLAS H. and VON PISCHKE, J.D. (Eds.): Undermining Rural Development with Cheap Credit, Boulder.*

WEBER, MAX (1923): Wirtschaftsgeschichte - Abriß der universalen Sozial- und Wirtschafts-Geschichte, München.

YELLEN, J.L. (1984): Efficiency Wage Models of Unemployment, in: The American Economic Review, Vol. 74, No. 2, May 1984, pp. 200-205.

Entwicklung und Finanzierung
Development and Finance

Herausgegeben von / Edited by
Reinhard H. Schmidt
Claus-Peter Zeitinger

Bd./Vol. 1 Heike Proff: Auswirkungen der Politik der internationalen Finanzinstitutionen (IWF und Weltbank) auf importintensive und exportorientierte Unternehmen in Ghana. 1994.

Bd./Vol. 2 Martin Holtmann / Rochus Mommartz: Technical Guide for Analyzing the Efficiency of Credit-Granting / Non-Governmental Organizations (NGOs). 1996.

Band 1 + 2 sind im Verlag für Entwicklungspolitik Breitenbach GmbH, Saarbrücken, erschienen und auch von dort zu beziehen.
Vol. 1 + 2 have already been published by Verlag für Entwicklungspolitik, Breitenbach GmbH, Saarbrücken, and are obtainable through the publishers.

Entwicklung und Finanzierung
Development and Finance

Herausgegeben von / Edited by
Manfred Nitsch, Reinhard H. Schmidt und Claus-Peter Zeitinger

Bd./Vol. 3 Ilonka Rühle: Why Banks? Microeconomic Foundations of Financial Intermediaries. 1997.

Bd./Vol. 4 Manfred Kiefer: Die Rentenreform in Peru. Auswirkungen auf soziale Sicherung, Finanzmärkte und Staatsfinanzen. 1998.

Bd./Vol. 5 Modibo Khane Camara: Die Finanzsektorreform in Afrika. Das Beispiel der Franc-Zone. 1998.

Bd./Vol. 6 Andreas Hackethal: Banken, Unternehmensfinanzierung und Finanzsysteme. 2000.

Bd./Vol. 7 Silvio Andrae / Kathrin Pingel: Tropical Finance. Von den (Un-)Möglichkeiten eines ländlichen Finanzsystems im brasilianischen Amazonien. 2001.

Bd./Vol. 8 Marcel Gounot: The Efficiency of Multi-Tier Savings and Credit Cooperatives in Developing Countries. A Study Based on Empirical Research in West Africa. 2001.

Bd/Vol. 9 Christian M. Pfeil: Capital Structure, Managerial Incentives and Corporate Governance. 2002.

Bd/Vol. 10 Sofia Harrschar-Ehrnborg: Finanzplatzstrukturen in Europa. Die Entstehung und Entwicklung von Finanzzentren. 2002.

Bd/Vol. 11 Ingo Tschach: The Theory of Development Finance. How Microcredit Programmes Alleviate Credit and Labour Market Segmentation. 2002.

Peter Lang · Europäischer Verlag der Wissenschaften

Hans-Rimbert Hemmer / Rainer Wilhelm

Fighting Poverty in Developing Countries

Principles for Economic Policy

Frankfurt/M., Berlin, Bern, Bruxelles, New York, Oxford, Wien, 2000.
XV, 242 pp., 7 fig., 16 tab.
Schriften zur Internationalen Entwicklungs- und Umweltforschung.
Herausgegeben vom Zentrum für internationale Entwicklungs- und Umweltforschung der Justus-Liebig-Universität Gießen. Bd. 1
ISBN 3-631-37145-4 · pb. € 40.40*/ US-$ 42.95 / £ 27.00
US-ISBN 0-8204-4824-9

Poverty is one of the most depressing facts in the world today. This book is written in order to provide a new perspective to the problem of poverty and to the discussion of anti-poverty policies in developing countries, including aspects of child labour and systemic transition, which are currently at the center of political debate. The intention of the book is to provide a common base for discussion for those professionals in developed, as well as those in developing countries. The authors hope that this book will be of use to those professionally occupied with these problems as well as to those "only" interested in issues of development economics.

Contents: Foundation of an economic analysis of poverty · The economic causes of poverty · Principles of anti-poverty policies · Points of departure and problems in the fight against poverty · Special issues in the fight against poverty

Frankfurt/M · Berlin · Bern · Bruxelles · New York · Oxford · Wien
Auslieferung: Verlag Peter Lang AG
Jupiterstr. 15, CH-3000 Bern 15
Telefax (004131) 9402131

*inklusive der in Deutschland gültigen Mehrwertsteuer
Preisänderungen vorbehalten

Homepage http://www.peterlang.de